EXPLAINING INEQUALITY

Inequalities in incomes and wealth have increased in advanced countries, making our economies less dynamic, our societies more unjust and our political processes less democratic. As a result, reducing inequalities is now a major economic, social and political challenge. This book provides a concise yet comprehensive overview of the economics of inequality.

Until recently economic inequality has been the object of limited research efforts, attracting only modest attention in the political arena. Despite important advances in the knowledge of its dimensions, a convincing understanding of the mechanisms at its roots is still lacking. This book summarises the topic and provides an interpretation of the mechanisms responsible for increased disparities. Building on this analysis the book argues for an integrated set of policies to address the roots of inequalities in incomes and wealth.

Explaining Inequality will be of interest to students, researchers and practitioners concerned with inequality, economic and public policy and political economy.

Maurizio Franzini is Full Professor of Economic Policy, Sapienza University of Rome, Italy.

Mario Pianta is Full Professor of Economic Policy, University of Urbino, Italy.

EXPLAINING INEQUALITY

Maurizio Franzini and Mario Pianta

Routledge
Taylor & Francis Group

LONDON AND NEW YORK

First published 2016
by Routledge
2 Park Square, Milton Park, Abingdon, Oxon OX14 4RN

and by Routledge
711 Third Avenue, New York, NY 10017

Routledge is an imprint of the Taylor & Francis Group, an informa business

British Library Cataloguing in Publication Data
A catalogue record for this book is available from the British Library

Library of Congress Cataloging in Publication Data
   Franzini, M. (Maurizio), 1950-
   Explaining inequality / Maurizio Franzini and Mario Pianta. — First Edition
      pages cm
   Includes bibliographical references and index.
   1. Income distribution. 2. Equality. 3. International economic integration.
   I. Pianta, Mario, 1956- II. Title.
   HB523.F738 2015
   339.2--dc23   2015023435

ISBN: 978-0-415-70349-9 (hbk)
ISBN: 978-0-415-70348-2 (pbk)
ISBN: 978-1-315-73445-3 (ebk)

Typeset in Bembo
by Sunrise Setting Ltd, Paignton, UK

CONTENTS

ILLUSTRATIONS

FIGURES

TABLE

1

FOUR ENGINES OF INEQUALITY

1.1 Introduction[1]

In the last 30 years the economic conditions of people in our societies have become more unequal – the rich have become much richer, the middle have lost ground, the poor have slipped behind. Whether we measure economic inequality in terms of income or wealth, we find that inequality within advanced countries has dramatically increased; disparities in income have indeed returned to levels typical of a century ago. Also, at the global level inequality remains extremely high despite the rapid growth of major developing countries such as China and India – where domestic disparities are booming.

This makes inequality a major economic issue, social problem and political challenge in today's capitalism. A growing attention has gone to studies of inequality – including bestseller books by Joseph Stiglitz (2012) and Thomas Piketty (2013) – but a convincing understanding of the mechanisms at the roots is still lacking. Therefore, inequality is far from becoming a sustained focus of social mobilisation, a priority for political forces, a major government concern.

Public opinion is indeed shocked to learn that by 2016 the richest 1 per cent of the world may own the same wealth as all the other human beings put together (Oxfam, 2015), but how can a link between such gross injustice and people's actual condition be made? The factors that have led to such an outcome remain out of the grasp of public opinion; is there a way this could ever be changed? In spite of occasional street demonstrations against the '1 per cent', no political strategy for reversing such trends is at hand.

Mainstream thinking has long argued that economic inequality is a necessary condition – or, at best, an unfortunate side effect – for achieving the more general objectives of economic growth and market efficiency. Why should we then be concerned with high inequality?

Even if we do become concerned, we are told that inequality is to a large extent the consequence of international or global forces, lying beyond the reach of nation-states, the political unit where policy measures for countering inequality have usually been implemented. Indeed, the forces shaping inequality a century ago were mainly rooted in the distribution of income within national economies. Today, they tend to be, to a significant extent, global processes – increased cross-border flows of capitals, goods, workers and knowledge; the expansion of finance; the rise and fall of industries and specialisations; international production by multinational firms; wage setting influenced by distant locations and so on. The ability of national policies to address such developments has greatly diminished and governments have apparently chosen to accept their powerlessness and to make their citizens learn to live with high inequality, rather than striving to understand and counter the forces of inequality and their most unacceptable outcomes. Moreover, no international political authority has emerged with the mandate to address and regulate the unequal outcomes of such cross-border processes.

Finally, we are told that the patterns of inequality show an unprecedented complexity; they are different from the past, include multiple dimensions – income and wealth, work and class, gender and ethnicity, education and social conditions, individual capacities and behaviour and so on. Such complexity is hard to understand and even harder to act upon; how can we be sure that policies can improve one aspect without at the same time worsening disparities in another dimension?

Such arguments need to be taken into account, but are no reason to give up on understanding inequality and on trying to reverse it. For most of the twentieth century the roots of inequality were in the transition from agricultural to industrial societies, in the resulting class structure and in the functional distribution of income between capital and labour. Today, finance is a dominating force in most economies, reshaping capital accumulation and the patterns of distribution of income and wealth. Firms are engaged in international production, experience greater competition and unequal economic fortunes. Labour markets are increasingly segmented and workers are divided by gender, between white and blue collars, knowledge and manual workers, permanent and temporary employees, local and migrant labour, not to mention the various forms of unemployment.

A century ago the class structure of societies could broadly account for inequalities in incomes, status and opportunities. Today class identities are blurred, inequalities within workers are deeper and new aspects play a role. The inequality experienced by individuals is shaped by a combination of factors including class, gender and ethnic status, education and professional skills, type of employment contracts, access to social rights and public services and opportunities for social mobility within and between generations. In the past, being a member of a social group, in particular of the class of workers rather than of capitalists, was enough to make a reliable prediction as to one's position in the social ladder. Today, individuals' positions are the result of a variety of factors; new mechanisms shape the economic conditions of particular groups and inequality within members of relatively homogenous social categories may be high. This overlapping of dimensions of inequality – with individuals located at different intersections of such characteristics – indeed results in greater complexity that defies old approaches to inequality. Such complexity may have discouraged academic research, social mobilisation and policy action.

This book aims to provide an explanation of today's high inequality – focusing on its economic dimension – which is parsimonious enough to identify the fundamental mechanisms at work and, at the same time, capable of accounting for its complexity. We argue that the following four forces are at the root of current economic inequality.

1.2 The four engines of inequality

The power of capital over labour

For advanced countries all the available evidence points to a turning point in the early 1980s in inequality dynamics. The arrival in power of Margaret Thatcher in the UK in 1979 and of Ronald Reagan in the US in 1980 has ushered in the age of neoliberalism, with political power captured by forces ready to break with the widely shared post-war Keynesian consensus on capital controls, wage bargaining with strong unions and an active role of the State in redistribution of incomes and provision of welfare services. One after another, advanced countries aligned to a view of markets as efficient tools not just to allocate resources, but also to distribute rewards. Liberalisation and deregulation became priorities in all fields of the economy and society; relatively closed economies were opened up by liberalised trade and capital flows.

The rise of finance was the most important process. The 1970s were a decade of severe crisis of the post-war order, characterised by mass production in 'Fordist' industries, with labour and social movements contesting the power of capital at all levels. In advanced countries the response of capital was a move towards finance, offering a new faster rate of capital accumulation. The banking regulations introduced after the Great Depression of the 1930s were progressively cancelled, the free international movement of capital was allowed (making, by the way, managed exchange rate systems impossible) and entire new fields of financial activities were opened up for business (future markets, currency trading, derivatives, hedge funds, trading in food, commodities, carbon, etc.) with a huge potential for growth of asset values and for short-term speculation. A decade later, in advanced countries, globalisation – in parallel with the accelerating diffusion of information and communication technologies – was reshaping production systems and technology and investment flows, weakening domestic production, destroying jobs, breaking union power and lowering wages.

The new power of capital over labour since the 1980s is responsible for the shift of at least 10 percentage points of gross domestic product (GDP) from the wage share to the capital share in advanced countries. It accounts for the even greater rise of wealth inequality driven by mounting values of financial assets. It explains the unprecedented rise of top incomes, which combine unheard-of compensations of managers, larger profits and capital gains from financial and real estate assets. The ratio of compensation of managers in the top 350 US firms to those of average employees rose from 30:1 in 1978, to 383:1 in 2000, to 296:1 in 2013 (Mishel and Davis, 2014) and reflects in a very effective way the new power of capital over labour.

Oligarch capitalism

An inequality that is driven by the extreme rise of top incomes – typically the richest 1 per cent in the US, the richest 5 per cent in some European countries – brings with it features that remind us of the *ancien régime*. A new 'aristocracy of money' concentrates wealth in a way that was long forgotten. The maintenance and extension of the stock of such wealth take priority over the growth of the flows of incomes. The result – as shown by Piketty (2013) – is a growing capital/income ratio and an ever growing concentration of rewards to capital in economies that may record slower GDP growth. The way such concentrated wealth is obtained is less and less the result of competitive processes, Schumpeterian innovations and market success. More and more it has to do with monopoly rents, protection from competition, bubbles in real estate and financial markets. The 'super rich' increasingly have the features of 'oligarchs', whose wealth is derived from power and privilege – political protection, monopoly position and acquisition of privatised public companies – rather than from economic success. As with the pay of most top managers, there is no special economic 'merit' in being part of the oligarchy. Moreover, concentrated wealth is transmitted over time within families – another element typical of the *ancien régime* – and the importance of wealth acquired through inheritance rises in all advanced countries (Piketty and Zucman, 2014b). In such an 'oligarch capitalism' the inter-generational transmission of inequality becomes more severe, the possibility of social mobility collapses and the link between economic 'merit' and distributional reward becomes irrelevant – as shown by Franzini *et al.* (2014). Some traits of this model – such as the importance of relationships over merit for finding jobs or for obtaining higher wages – are spreading down through the system with a dangerous search for privilege over competence. As already argued – among others by Stiglitz (2012) – such a pattern of extreme inequality leads to lower economic efficiency and lower growth. Even more worrying is the prospect that this oligarch power may increasingly affect the political process, shaping public policy in their own interest and leading to a dramatic weakening of democratic systems.

Individualisation

The rising power of capital and 'oligarch capitalism' are engines of inequalities at the top of the distribution; they distance the 'top' from the rest and – even more – from the poorest. But inequalities have increased also within the '99 per cent'. The fundamental mechanism here is a process of individualisation that has put employees in competition with one another for pay and career; has led to a polar-isation of skills; and has pushed professionals and the self-employed in increasingly competitive markets. Individualisation has meant that workers in general have more precarious jobs with a great variety of contractual positions – short-term, part-time, outsourced jobs – while young people have increasingly uncertain and diversified professional trajectories. Outside employment, pensioners have also come to rely on differentiated pensions systems dependent from financial markets for their income. When we consider the way individuals are grouped in households, additional com-plexities emerge.

For people in employment these dynamics have led to a polarisation of jobs on the basis of professional categories and skills, bringing with it a frequent polarisa-tion of wages. This accounts for the large share of earnings inequality not explained by skills and education, but rather by family background or relational activities. The generalised weakening of trade unions and centralised labour contracts has removed the most powerful force for convergence in labour incomes and for supporting wage dynamics; this has opened up space for firm-level bargaining and individual contracts that have increased disparities among wage earners. Policy changes have directly contributed to this outcome with a general reduction in the degree of employment protection by legal norms (see Bogliacino and Maestri, 2014; Salverda and Checchi, 2014).

The complexity that has been documented in the patterns of inequality that concern the '99 per cent' is the result of such factors. In fast-changing produc-tion systems – affected by technological change, globalisation and evolution of skill structures – wage disparities have increased. Labour market institutions have also changed, with a lower degree of protection for employees and a fragmentation of contractual arrangements, leading to further inequalities among workers.

This is a process that goes well beyond incomes and wages. Social identities have indeed become more fragmented, class structures have become blurred and new divisions have emerged. The neoliberal emphasis on individuals, their choices and opportunities, has come a long way in also shaping broad social behaviour among workers. Traditional mechanisms creating collective identi-ties and a sense of solidarity – trade unionism for employees of the same indus-try and firm, community activism at the local level, etc. – have been weakened by an individualisation that can be seen as an additional, deeper sign of the new power of capital over labour.

The retreat of politics

Until the 1970s in advanced countries the State has played a major role in reduc-ing inequalities with a wide range of activities and policies. Income distribution was governed by overall policies concerning incomes policy, taxation, rent con-trols, the regulation of finance and capital flows. Disparities emerging from market outcomes were contained by a highly progressive tax system, by selective taxes discouraging conspicuous consumption, by high inheritance taxes and by extensive provision of public services outside the market; income support was provided for the less fortunate.

Since the 1980s almost all of these policies have been outright cancelled – as in the case of the inheritance tax in many countries – or substantially weakened – as for progressive taxation. Public policies took the road of market liberalisation and deregulation, favouring in all possible ways the new power of capital over labour and the rise of finance. Politics made it possible for capital to break the resistance of labour and for finance to become the leading industry of our time. Policies were introduced to change an endless list of 'rules of the game' in the name of market efficiency and reduction of 'public waste'. Private enterprise was encouraged, private finance was favoured even more, new markets were opened up, public activities privatised – and, sometimes, handed over to 'oligarch capitalists' – regulations were reduced. This neoliberal landscape was progressively introduced and spread all over advanced countries.

Until the 1970s the role of State action in reducing inequalities was much broader than the setting of the rules and the 'correction' of market outcomes. The large-scale provision – especially in Europe – of public services through non-market systems – including education, health, social security, pensions, environmental protection, public research and development (R&D), etc. – meant that the operation of markets, with their drive towards unequal outcomes – was limited and that people could access such services on the basis of their status as equal citizens rather than on the basis of their (unequal) ability to pay. This has been a powerful equalising factor from the 1950s to the 1970s in all advanced countries.

Moreover, in many European countries State intervention was also widespread in economic activities, with public enterprises managing infrastructures, water, energy and communications, as well as large firms in a range of key industries from steel to electronics. When economic activities are carried out by publicly owned organisations – either public agencies or firms – profits either do not exist or end up as State revenue, reducing taxation; in any case they do not increase the capital share or the importance of finance. State management has to aim at efficiency and effectiveness, not to maximum profits and workers in publicly owned organisations are usually granted good wages, greater union rights and employment protection under labour contracts that tend to equalise conditions. In the case of public firms operating alongside private enterprises in the same industry, this has also an effect on the wages and conditions found in private firms, as well as on the possibility to avoid collusive practices, excessive market power and price increases.

Since the 1980s, the drive towards privatisation of public firms and of public services, and the outsourcing of service provision to private organisations – firms and non-profit organisations – has integrated a large part of such activities in market contexts, breaking all conditions that had limited inequalities in such activities; in fact, some of the lowest wages are now paid in the outsourcing of formerly public services.

As documented by a wide range of studies – in particular Atkinson (2015) – the impact on inequality of such a retreat of politics has been huge. Disparities have increased with both a 'distancing' of the rich and a 'falling behind' of the poor.

The failure of policies to contain inequalities has led to some of the most visible and problematic effects – increasing poverty, social deprivation, even a reduction of the years of life expectancy for the poorer in many countries (Therborn, 2013).

It should be noted that these four forces of inequality operate at different levels but closely interact with one another, reinforcing their effects. A strengthening of capital versus labour makes possible the introduction of anti-labour and anti-poor policies that further consolidate unbalanced class relations. The individualisation of workers' positions in labour markets is closely associated to a strengthening of capital's power over labour. A more individualised society offers less resistance to the rise of the wealth and power of oligarchs. A concentration of wealth in the hands of oligarchs means greater influence over the policy process that further advances their privilege and rents. The reduction of the public sphere through privatisations and deregulation widens the space where the polarising effect of market dynamics operates.

Indeed, these intertwined mechanisms are a further reflection of the complexity of today's inequality and are part of the broader model of neoliberal capitalism that has emerged since the 1980s. However, it is important to separate each of the four forces of inequality because they are characterised by specific dynamics, operate at separate levels and different policies are required to reverse them.

The explanation we propose for today's inequality is developed in the rest of this chapter with an overview of the changing views of inequality in economic studies and a summary of why inequality matters.

1.3 Changing views of inequality

Economic inequality is a changing phenomenon; its forces evolve over time and even similar levels of disparities may be the results of different mechanisms and patterns of distribution. Economic ideas on inequality have evolved accordingly.

For Classical economists, inequality was defined by the class structure of industrial capitalism and by the distribution of income between capital and labour. The relationships between patterns of distribution, economic growth and social reproduction were a key concern in their analysis industrialisation.

Marx emphasised the contradiction between industrial capitalism's potential for progress and its outcome – capital accumulation for the capitalist class, and commodified labour, limited wages and hard social conditions for workers and the dispossessed. Increasing inequalities – relative to the poorer, but more equal, pre-industrial societies – were the result of the very nature of capitalist accumulation.

Problems of distribution and inequalities 'disappeared' in neoclassical approaches behind widely accepted – and surprisingly long-living – assumptions. At the macroeconomic level, the compensation of factors of production was assumed to be equal to their marginal productivity; at the individual level, incomes were simply the result of choices on work, investment and consumption that resulted from individual utilities. Freedom of choice and market efficiency could justify any (unequal) distributional outcome, with no consequence for economic growth and no room for the principles of social justice, human rights nor for redistributive policies. The Great Depression of the 1930s proved how unrealistic such assumptions were and how disastrous were their policy implications.

In the post-war period, the link between income distribution and growth returned at the centre of Keynesian approaches, with two distinct mechanisms: on the demand side, wages were seen as a major source of aggregate demand; on the supply side, accumulation – financed by profits and savings – was needed to expand productive capacities. The main concern of Kaldorian models (Kaldor, 1956) and post-Keynesian perspectives (Robinson, 1960) was to identify the distributive patterns that were consistent with sustained growth, recognising a major role for government action in supporting both accumulation and demand – through public expenditure and redistribution that could support the lowest incomes and reduce inequality. Moreover, insights from welfare economics informed the normative models for economic policy aiming at redistribution, pointing out the trade-offs between efficiency and equity in static and dynamic contexts.

The empirical regularities of such processes were pointed out by Kuznets (1965), who suggested the inverted-U relationship between levels of inequality and countries' per capita income; industrialisation and growth would first increase inequalities – as a result of the structural change from low to high productivity sectors – which would then decline as a result of the diffusion of industry, redistribution and more balanced growth.

Indeed, Europe and the US experienced a reduction in inequalities from the 1950s to the 1970s as a result of economic growth, social change and public policies for redistribution and welfare. One of the side effects – as repeatedly argued by Atkinson (2015) – was that for several decades inequality became a rarely explored field of economic research, with few specialised studies.

A new attention has emerged since the 1990s, following the new rise in inequality that had started in the 1980s. Such studies have moved from the functional distribution of income between social classes to inequalities among individuals. The argument was that class divisions had become less clear cut, and gender, ethnicity, education and professional qualifications had become major factors in explaining the personal distribution of income. A large number of detailed studies have addressed these issues, documenting more complex patterns of inequality among individuals and households (Atkinson and Bourguignon, 2000, 2014a; Salverda *et al.*, 2009, 2014). This approach, however, largely missed the continuing importance of capital–labour relationships and the new key role of top incomes combining rents, profits and unprecedented high compensations for top managers (Atkinson and Piketty, 2007; Atkinson *et al.*, 2011). What we are facing today – after the temporary reduction of disparities between 1950 and 1980 – is a return to the levels of inequalities of a century ago. Kuznets's curve has indeed been reversed.

In parallel, the rapid accumulation of financial and real estate assets by the richest individuals has attracted attention to inequalities in *wealth,* and an emerging stream of research is now exploring wealth disparities and their link to inequalities in incomes (Piketty, 2013; Piketty and Zucman, 2014b; Maestri *et al.*, 2014).

Building on the evidence of the growing shares of profits and financial rents and on the increasing concentration of income and wealth, Piketty (2013) has argued that the roots of growing inequality are in returns to capital that are greater than the growth rate of the economy, leading to an increasing capital/income ratio – two fundamental mechanisms of capitalism (see the discussion in chapter 4).

Other attempts to explain growth in inequality in advanced countries have focused on disparities within wages in the context of globalisation and techno-logical change. A large literature within the economic mainstream has argued that the rising wages of highly skilled white collars reflected the greater labour productivity of workers capable of using the new information and communica-tion technologies and that wage inequalities were the result of *skill biased technical change* (Acemoglu, 2002). These studies ignored that advanced countries were not experiencing a generalised 'upskilling' of jobs, from blue- to white-collar employ-ment, but rather a polarisation was taking place with more jobs for managers and professionals and for the lowest skills – manual workers and ancillary jobs. Losses in jobs and wages were concentrated among office clerks (the low-skilled white col-lars) and skilled factory workers (the most qualified blue-collar employees) (Nascia and Pianta, 2009; Cirillo *et al.*, 2014). While technological change does have an impact on inequality, it is arguably more complex than the *skill bias* view, as recently acknowledged also by mainstream views (Acemoglu and Autor, 2010). Moreover, these effects are combined with increasing foreign trade and investment that have a parallel, often overlapping, impact on changes in employment, skills and wages in advanced economies (Feenstra and Hanson, 2003).

Higher wage inequality has also been explained with developments in labour markets, where the changing balance of power between capital and labour has led to the rapid rise of temporary and precarious jobs, the fall of unionisation and of trade union influence and a greater fragmentation of labour, including the effects of education, part-time contracts, greater women's participation, migrations, etc. (ILO, 2015; OECD, 2015; Checchi and Garcia-Penalosa, 2008; Salverda and Checchi, 2014). Such developments have been summarised as labour's 'defeat' in income distribution (Glyn, 2006, 2009).

Today's inequality in advanced countries is therefore the result of a set of dif-ferent and complex mechanisms. While extensive empirical evidence has been provided (Atkinson and Bourguignon, 2000, 2014a; Salverda *et al.*, 2009, 2014), a convincing explanation of the 'engines of inequality' is still lacking. It has to com-bine the importance of the functional distribution of income between capital and labour, the growing role of finance in creating disparities, the rise of top incomes and the new complexity of the personal and household distribution, where indi-viduals' and families' incomes are shaped by education, skills, gender and ethnicity, as well as class. Moreover, the growing importance of the expansion of wealth – in finance and in real estate – has introduced a major change in the functioning of advanced economies and in their patterns of distribution.

Inequality is also important because it is reproduced across generations. For a long time, studies on advanced countries have assumed that improved education and the end of rigid class divides offered higher equality of opportunities and greater social mobility. More recent studies, however, have disputed such views with evidence that inequality persists from one generation to the next, and that (apparently) more equal opportunities do not reduce unequal outcomes in income distribution among individuals (OECD, 2008, 2011; Franzini and Raitano, forthcoming).

At the same time, philosophical and economic perspectives have addressed the issues of justice, ethics, equality of opportunities and inter-generational inequality. Liberal theories of justice stated the primacy of individuals' freedom of choice and explored the possibilities of reducing inequality without limiting liberty. Rawls (1971) argued that, in a society made of rational, self-interested individuals, a majority would accept a redistribution that improves the position of the worse-off in a society. An emphasis on equality of opportunities – as opposed to equality of outcomes – has characterised recent conceptualisations, as in Roemer (1998). Moving beyond such models, Amartya Sen has pointed out the complexity of inequality, rooted in societies' historical contexts, in the capabilities available to people, families and social groups in the pursuit of their objectives and in the concrete opportunities that individuals have to make decisions about their lives (Sen, 1992, 2009).

From his work we derive that the 'equality of capabilities to function as human beings' appears as the most convincing ethical foundation for the desirability of equality. Typically, life protection and health, access to education and knowledge and freedom of choice appear as human rights that should be granted equally to all. The UN Human Development Index is based on such a conceptualisation and ranks countries on the basis of an average of their life expectancy, educational levels and GDP per capita; additional indicators have been developed in this perspective, highlighting the human right dimensions of global inequalities (UNDP, 2014).

These approaches have moved together with a broader recognition that inequality cannot be confined to incomes and economic factors, and that access to education and health, as well as social conditions, play a key role in shaping (unequal) life prospects for individuals. While incomes appear to be highly related to several of these social conditions, a wider conceptualisation of inequality is needed. Therborn (2013) has argued that there are three (interconnected) types of inequality: vital inequality (shown by life expectancy and health conditions), existential inequality (documented by differences across classes, status, gender and ethnicity) and resource inequality (the one economists are mostly concerned with). He also identified the mechanisms of 'distanciation', exclusion, hierchisation and exploitation that shape inequalities of all types, organising what really is a 'socio-cultural order' not just a diversity of income and wealth (Therborn, 2013: 53, 63, 1).

In fact, a lot can be learned from studies on social and health conditions. Therborn reports impressive data on the persistence of vital inequalities in life expectancy:

> Between the 33 boroughs of London the range of male life expectancy has widened from 5.4 years in 1999–2001 to 9.2 years in 2006–2008. If you travel east on the underground Jubilee line, life expectancy of the residents is decreasing by half a year at every stop.
>
> *(Therborn, 2013: 82, quoting the London Health Observatory, 2011)*

Wilkinson and Pickett (2009) have shown that higher inequalities in advanced countries are associated to a full range of social problems – from suicides to drug use, from prison population to obesity – contributing to shortening the life expectancy of the poor. Moreover, they also found preliminary evidence that living in contexts of high inequality is bad *even for the rich,* as even oligarchs can hardly shield themselves from a number of pervasive social ills in the society where they live. In the study of such dimensions of inequality, the need for greater interdisciplinarity, with collaboration between economists, sociologists, political scientists, statisticians, epidemiologists and philosophers, is by now widely accepted, but not yet practised enough.

The context in which inequality can be investigated has also evolved, moving from national to international perspectives. World income inequalities between countries and regions have been investigated in their evolution over time and space; approaches have first focused on differences among countries (considering their average per capita income), combining them with inequalities among individuals within a country. Greater efforts are now made to estimate global inequality among all the world population, regardless of countries (Milanovic, 2005, 2011, 2012; Lakner and Milanovic, 2013; Cornia, 2004). When the relevance of the incomes of the richest 1 per cent is considered, the evidence shows that in the last decades inequality has increased also among the world population as a whole, in spite of the 'equalising effect' of higher average income in (highly unequal) emerging countries such as China and India (Anand and Segal, 2014). Key determinants of the changing world income distribution have been identified in the different phases of countries' development, in the global flows of knowledge, trade and finance, and in countries' positions in the core or periphery of the world system (Arrighi, 1991). These studies contributed to the debate on the distribution of the benefits of globalisation and questioned the economic rationale, the social sustainability and the political acceptability of extremely wide income inequalities at the global level.

1.4 Why inequality matters

The focus of this book is a comprehensive explanation of the nature of economic inequality in today's capitalism. We investigate key mechanisms and their inter-relations, while leaving the consequences of inequality – economic, social and political – on the side of our analysis. But behind the question 'Why does inequality increase?' there is the deeper question 'Why does inequality matter?', and we need to address it briefly because this issue, too, has become more difficult and complex in recent decades.

Liberal perspectives have long argued that 'equality of opportunities' is what matters and that disparities following from such a condition are socially acceptable and economically efficient. In other words, 'this inequality does not matter', from an ethical, political or economic viewpoint. Extensive evidence shows that advanced economies in the last decades have remained far from granting equal opportunities, and that the liberal justification is supported by little evidence on the economic benefits in terms of faster growth that can be associated to high inequality. The point we want to raise here, however, goes beyond such traditional argument and focuses on the novelty of today's inequality. In fact, the new nature of today's inequality is changing the frame of the debate in at least three aspects.

First, today's inequality is largely shaped by the extreme rise of top incomes – earning profits, financial rents and very high compensations – with an increasingly polarised pattern of distribution of incomes and wealth. This is associated with a collapse in the opportunities for education-driven social mobility and with a rise of the persistence of inequalities across generations. Economic privilege is becoming more extreme and is increasingly inherited – a return to a feature of inequality that was typical of a century ago. An inequality of such nature has important consequences on the economy and society. In economic terms, the 'neoclassical' argument that inequality may contribute to faster economic growth by rewarding individuals with higher merit and capacities loses whatever is left of its credibility as the incomes and wealth of the richest people are less the result of successful business growth (that may benefit the whole economy) and more the outcome of financial speculation and family privilege (a net burden on the economy). Conversely, the entrepreneurial efforts of middle- and low-income individuals are likely to be reduced by the lower prospects of social mobility. In social terms, these developments are hollowing the meaning of 'equality of opportunities' and the mechanisms of social mobility and change; society is shaped by more rigid social hierarchies, with features typical of a 'feudal' society – including the growing number of people employed in the personal service of the very rich. This new nature of inequality matters because it cannot be justified even by the traditional liberal argument, and may have highly negative effects on the economic and social prospects of countries.

Second, we show in this book that the mechanisms producing inequality in advanced countries have become more complex – investing the overall patterns of distribution as well as type of education, position in employment, family background, etc. – and this is likely to produce economic and social outcomes characterised by a much greater fragmentation along class, status, gender, education and local conditions. Individuals' and families' incomes are likely to be determined by a greater variety of factors on which they have less and less control. It not just the high *level* of inequality that may threaten social cohesion. This new nature of inequality matters because the diversity of processes increase the effects on disparities of outcomes and social fragmentation, with higher uncertainty and sense of powerlessness of an ever larger share of people posing a more serious danger to social cohesion and stability of countries. In turn, the complexity of these mechanisms makes policy responses to high inequality more difficult and less effective.

Third, the economic and social conditions that define specific patterns of inequality are shaped by a complex frame defined by political institutions – supranational and national – and by the political processes leading to policy making and redistribution. While we usually think of such 'frames' as 'neutral' and independent from a given pattern of inequality, they in fact can be heavily affected by highly unequal societies, further exacerbating disparities.

Several contributions have explored this issue. The 'radical democratic' approach proposed by Nancy Fraser (2005) defines justice as 'parity of participation' and identifies unjust outcomes in three cases: when economic inequality leads to distributive injustice; when social hierarchies and cultural values lead to status inequalities and lack of 'recognition'; and when political structures – global and national – lead to a lack of equal representation. The latter are particularly important as they 'frame' the way distribution and recognition issues can be addressed by the political process.

Addressing global inequalities and world poverty, Pogge (2002) suggests that today's world is characterised by 'radical inequality', defined as follows: the conditions of the worse-off are very bad both in absolute and relative terms; they have little or no possibility to overcome a hardship pervading all their lives; and the inequality is avoidable, as redistribution could improve the conditions of the worse-off without worsening too much those of better-off. A key factor in shaping such radical inequality at the global level are global institutional rules that, far from being 'neutral', are the result of the balance of interests and political power of the different actors involved, with a dominant role of the interests of rich countries and of the élites of poor countries. Once the rules are set, given the unequal economic and political resources, it may become very difficult to change them through the political process. In this way, according to Pogge, inequality matters because it affects the public debate and policy making, preventing a return to low inequality arrangements and becoming therefore irreversible.

The relevance of institutional frameworks, and the influence of high inequality on political and economic outcomes, has also been emphasised by Wade (2004) for inequalities at the global level, and by Pontusson (2005) – following the 'varieties of capitalisms' approach – in the comparison between the US and European models. The case of the US – with its high inequality and overwhelming political influence of the rich – has been explored by Stiglitz (2012, 2015), Phillips (2003), Bartels (2008) and Hacker and Pierson (2010), who have pointed out the dangerous effects on the functioning of democratic processes, on political equality and policy outcomes that systematically favour high-income groups, further deepening inequality.

These different contributions reach the common conclusion that inequality matters because it affects the institutional setting and the political process – at the global and national levels – leading to a failure of democracy, to disparities in political rights and to 'irreversible inequality'.

These three dimensions of today's inequalities provide further evidence on the unacceptable nature of such disparities. They outline new ethical, political and economic answers to the question 'Why does inequality matter?' and support the need to address them with appropriate and comprehensive policy actions.

In this regard, the recent policy shift by international institutions, such as the Organisation for Economic Co-operation and Development (OECD) and the International Monetary Fund (IMF), is remarkable in that they have long justified policies at the root of the rise in inequality. The last OECD report on inequality argues that 'rising inequality is bad for long-term growth' and that 'structural policies are needed now more than ever … but have to be carefully designed and complemented by measures that promote a better distribution of the growth dividends' (OECD, 2015: 22). OECD policy advice to countries has long centred on 'pro-growth' policies based on market-oriented 'structural reforms' that have increased disparities; their negative effects on growth are now acknowledged.

A recent IMF Staff Note concludes that 'lower net inequality is robustly correlated with faster and more durable growth' and that 'redistribution appears generally benign in terms of its impact on growth' (Ostry *et al.*, 2014: 4). Other IMF research finds that 'if the income share of the top 20% (the rich) increases, then GDP growth actually declines over the medium term' (Dabla-Norris *et al.*, 2015: 4) and that the decline of unionisation is a major factor in rising income inequality (Jaumotte and Osorio Buitron, 2015). The IMF policy advice to countries has long been that growth had to be sustained by lower taxes and public expenditure aiming at redistribution and that unions were a major problem for the efficient operation of labour markets. These are encouraging signs that in advanced countries the policy consensus that has long supported pro-rich policies may be breaking down.

The following chapters explore all these issues in great detail and provide an overall interpretation of the engines of inequality that are at work in advanced countries. Chapter 2 investigates the various ways in which the power of capital over labour has been established, providing empirical evidence on the distribution of income between profits and wages and the market processes that shape disparities of income – of individuals and households, before and after taxes, redistribution and public services. It investigates the deeper inequalities in wealth and disparities at the global level.

Chapter 3 shows – again with extensive empirical evidence – that family relationships have a renewed importance in the reproduction of inequalities. This is obvious in the transmission of wealth through inheritance – with extreme situations in the case of oligarchs. It is less obvious in the distribution of rewards: family background is found to be more important than education and merit in several patterns of income distribution, including wage levels.

Chapter 4 provides the interpretation of the forces of inequality documented in previous chapters. The power of capital, oligarch capitalism, individualisation and the retreat of politics are examined from a conceptual perspective, with a review of relevant studies and evidence, weaving together the threads of a necessary explanation of inequality. As already argued, the first mechanism we identify is the power of capital over labour; it is rooted in the dynamics of capital accumulation in the age of finance and in the functional distribution of income that has led to the increasing divide between the growing share of profits and financial rents – free to move across national borders, escape taxation and search for speculative gains – and the dwindling share of wages. The second mechanism is that of 'oligarch capitalism', driven by the rise of top incomes – that combine rents, profits and extreme compensations – by the even stronger concentration of wealth and by mechanisms that reproduce inequality from one generation to the next through the importance of family, heritage and lack of social mobility. The third mechanism is the individualisation of relationships in the economy and society. This explains why inequalities have also strongly increased within wages, resulting from several factors. Education has an obvious influence, but, however, plays a much smaller role than mainstream views would expect. Skill differences are increasingly important, and need to be examined in the context of specific professional groups rather than with wide generalisations. Industry specificities, technology and international production do play a role, but in complex ways, depending on the nature of innovative strategies, local competences, market power and demand dynamics. Labour market arrangements – unionisation, presence of minimum wages or national contracts, diffusion of temporary or part-time labour contracts and so on, are increasingly important factors in explaining the low pay of many young and low-skilled workers.

Chapter 5 moves to the politics of inequality, addressing the fourth mechanism we identify – the retreat of politics. The redistributive effects of taxation, social incomes – pensions and transfers – and provision of public services provided outside the market shape inequalities among families in terms of net disposable incomes and standard of living. However, the reduced spending capacity of national governments, the weakening of progressive taxation, the ability of top incomes to escape taxation and the spreading privatisation of public services have all weakened the redistributive effects of public policies. The chapter argues that we need to reverse the 'retreat of politics' in front of inequality and identifies the new, widely shared and feasible policies – at the national, European and global level – that could reduce inequality in advanced economies and, in addition, move our countries out of the uncertainty and stagnation that has followed the crisis started in 2008.

The combination of these four 'engines of inequality' has returned advanced countries to the economic disparities of a century ago. The interpretation we provide offers a new explanation of the nature of today's economic inequality, of its consequences and possible remedies.

Note

1   This book draws on years of research, presentations at workshops and public discussion on inequality. Key ideas of this book are sketched in Franzini and Pianta (2009, 2011) and in our studies of inequality and economic crisis in Italy (Franzini, 2010, 2013; Pianta, 2012). The problems of high incomes and wealth are addressed in Franzini *et al.* (2014), the policy alternatives are discussed in Marcon and Pianta (2013). We thank Francesco Bogliacino, Valeria Cirillo, Elena Granaglia, Dario Guarascio, Matteo Lucchese and Michele Raitano for discussion on these issues.

2

CAPITAL, LABOUR AND THE DISTRIBUTION OF INCOME

2.1 Introduction

Inequality starts with the way the economy is organised and income is distributed. In this chapter we show that advanced countries during the last 30 years have been characterised by a major change in the patterns of distribution resulting from market outcomes: the share of income going to capital has increased and the share going to labour has fallen. This 'functional' distribution of income going to the 'factors of production' (capital and labour) can then be investigated in the way it reaches individuals and households – who can receive both capital and labour incomes – leading to the 'personal' distribution of income emerging from market outcomes. Household income, in turn, is modified by taxation and redistribution (pensions and welfare payments) leading to the distribution of disposable (monetary) income. The presence of non-market activities should be taken into account. When public services such as education and health are provided to all as a citizen right paid by taxation, they reach all individuals on the basis of their needs rather than on their ability to pay, exerting an important 'equalising' effect; disposable income can therefore be adjusted with the 'value' of in-kind services provided by the welfare state. In this way we can measure inequality among households after the effects of all available policies.

Inequality can increase as a result of different processes. In advanced countries the dominant pattern has been the rise of 'top incomes' – those of the richest 10 per cent or 1 per cent of the population – that have accelerated at an unprecedented rate, leaving behind the rest. They have typically combined high returns from financial investment and strong capital gains from the increased value of financial and real estate wealth. Top managers and other 'star' professionals have also obtained unprecedented compensations for their activities that combine a remuneration for their labour, a rent from their social and professional power and a share of the profits often delivered in the form of stock. It is on this process that the analysis of Piketty (2013) has focused.

What about the rest of the income distribution? The increased share of the richest 10 per cent has reduced the (relative) income of almost everyone else; in most advanced countries the poorest 10 or 20 per cent have indeed suffered major (absolute) losses of market incomes, while the 'middle' of the distribution has had a moderate loss or a stagnation of real incomes. Growing disparities in such market outcome distribution to individuals are reflected in a rise in inequality – with some variation across countries and periods – also among households where the different incomes received by their members are combined and adjustment for household size – including children and the elderly – is made through equivalence scales. Disparities in household 'equivalised' market income are reduced everywhere by the effect of taxes and transfers that result in household disposable income. An even greater reduction of inequality comes from the estimates of 'extended' household income that include the monetary value of imputed rents for home owners and of the provision of public services obtained outside the market. The bad news, however, is that in the last decades policy changes – less progressive taxation, reduced transfers and cuts in public services – have deeply weakened the redistributive processes. The result is that in most advanced countries inequality among households has continued to increase even after the effect of policy.

Typically, this is the approach to investigate inequality within a country; how can we measure inequality at the world level? When many countries are considered, we can measure inequalities among the average (or median) incomes of each economy, finding that in recent decades the rapid growth of emerging countries has reduced the distance from advanced ones. But countries have different sizes of population (China is a typical case) and such measures could be weighted by population size in order to have a more accurate picture. However, inequalities within China have increased dramatically, and the disparities within and among countries should be considered together. Ideally, we should have data on each person (or family) in the world and measure inequality in the world as a whole. As we will see in section 2.6, when we adopt such measures we find that world income inequalities have not been reduced.

How do the 'engines of inequality', discussed in chapter 1, affect such patterns of inequality? As expected, this happens in complex ways, and in this chapter we identify some of the major mechanisms. The distribution between capital and labour is shaped by the quantity and quality of both factors of production. Total profits will be higher when more capital is invested, new technologies are used and market structures allow oligopolistic power. A greater role of finance – as it has emerged in the last 30 years – would expand the share of profits (that pay financial rents also) because of the generally higher returns (and tax elusion and evasion) allowed by financial investments in unregulated global capital markets.

Total wages will be higher when the quantity of employment expands and when the composition of jobs shifts towards higher 'quality' – from agriculture to manufacturing, or from traditional to high-tech industries, where higher education and wages are needed. Conversely, total wages will be lower when jobs are moved abroad by international production systems, when they are replaced by machinery, when workers lose the protection of unions, national labour contracts and permanent employment, and when precarious, low-wage jobs expand.

In advanced countries the combination of these processes has resulted in a greater power of capital over labour, and in an unprecedented reduction in the labour share of total income. A more detailed investigation of how the 'engines of inequality' operate will be provided in chapter 4.

The third mechanism we have pointed out is the growing 'individualisation' of economic conditions in terms of employment relations, labour market outcomes, disposable income and access to social rights. Disparities among individuals have increased on the basis of different factors; labour markets have become more segmented on the basis on employment contracts, precarious jobs and the entry of migrants; the expected returns of education on wages have been moderated, while family background has gained influence in shaping actual income; social mobility based on merit has decreased; and positions of rent in particular activities have become more relevant, in spite of the persistent rhetoric on competition. These developments affect wage earners in complex ways and, in particular, the 'middle' of the distribution of income; their effect on overall inequality measures could be difficult to detect, but they increase the perception of unfairness of the distributional outcomes.

So far we have considered the annual *flows* of incomes to capital, labour and households, but the *stock* of wealth, which generates the stream of capital income, is equally important for understanding inequality. Piketty (2013) made a major contribution in drawing attention to the role of wealth. With the rise of finance, and frequent speculative 'bubbles' in the financial and real estate markets, the value of wealth has increased at a much faster pace than that of GDP, contributing to the rise of 'top incomes' and to greater income inequality. But wealth inequality – both at the national and at the global level – has indeed reached extreme, unacceptable levels and represents a major challenge for our societies. Too little attention has been devoted so far to wealth disparities and to their effects on growth and on the efficiency and fairness of economic activities. In particular, large wealth is transmitted through heritage from one generation to the next. With the drastic reduction or abolition of inheritance taxes in most advanced countries, such disparities are becoming ever more entrenched; as returns on wealth are greater than income growth, the possibility of accumulating wealth out of incomes is reduced, and the concentration of wealth is increasing through inheritance. Merit, education and efficiency are losing their role in the distribution of economic benefits over a lifetime, and today's capitalism becomes increasingly close to an *ancien régime* society dominated by an oligarchy of wealth (see chapter 3).

Large and growing disparities in wealth are both the result of and a factor contributing to the power of capital over labour, and are the driving force of 'oligarch capitalism', the first two engines of inequality we have identified in chapter 1.

This chapter provides evidence on the processes summarised above; chapter 3 will then focus on the role of families in inequalities of income and wealth, adding an inter-generational dimension. The interpretation of the sources of inequality will be developed in chapter 4. The fourth engine of inequality we identify, the 'retreat of politics', is examined in chapter 5 where the scope for new policies is discussed.

2.2 Capital vs. labour

Inequality between capital and labour is reflected in the functional distribution of income. In advanced countries, labour's share ranges between 55 and 70 per cent of national income; it had increased during the 1970s, and has fallen since the 1980s, shifting to capital between 10 and 15 percentage points of total income. Calculations differ depending on the variables used (GDP, net income or value added of the private sector) and on methodologies adopted (for treating the financial sector, capital consumption, income of self-employed, etc.). Data – in particular for the US and UK – show a substantial difference when the income of the top 1 per cent of wage earners – that mostly include top managers who receive a combination of capital and labour income – is excluded from labour income. Overall, employee compensation shows a modest decline since 1980, while compensation of the bottom 99 per cent of wage earners experiences a fall of close to 10 percentage points in the net value added of the business sector. A fundamental shift in capital–labour relations has emerged since the 1980s; profits have rebounded, financial rents have substantially increased, in a few countries a higher share has gone to the self-employed, and the wage share has fallen. The fall in labour's compensation is parallel to the rise in personal income inequality (Glyn, 2009: 122).

The ILO Global Wage Report 2014–2015 (ILO, 2015) provides an effective summary of such trends showing the impact of the crisis started in 2008. Figure 2.1 reports the pattern between 1991 and 2013 for major advanced countries members of the G20 group.[1] The measure is the labour share in income considering total labour compensation (wages and social insurance contributions paid by employers), adjusted for the income of the self-employed. The general fall of the labour share has continued. In 1991 shares ranged between 59 per cent (in France and Australia) to 66 per cent (in the UK and Japan); in 2013 they were below 60 per cent everywhere (with the exception of the UK) and as low as 55 per cent (in Italy and Australia). UK and US data may be biased upward by the presence within the labour share of 'labour income' by the top managers in the

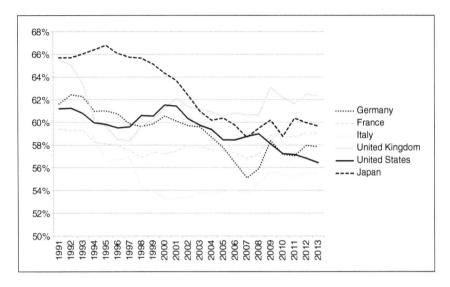

FIGURE 2.1 Labour income share in advanced countries, 1991–2013

Note: Wage share of GDP adjusted for the income of the self-employed (compensation per employee as a percentage of GDP at market prices per person employed). Data from European Commission AMECO database.

Source: Adapted from: *ILO Global Wage Report* 2014–15: 11 © 2015 International Labour Organization

richest 10 per cent. Italy, the US and Japan have been the countries with the steepest loss of labour income. In this general downward trend, the values for 2007 and 2008 have marked the lowest labour shares for all countries; the recession of 2009 has, as expected, hit profits most, but the rise of labour shares in that year has been followed by a new fall in 2010 for all countries and by modest changes in either direction since then.

A breakdown of such data shows that since the 1990s the falling labour share is not the result of shifts in the sectoral composition of the economy (from labour-intensive to capital-intensive sectors), but of greater profits within industries, especially in financial services and medium-high technology (ILO, 2015: 11; 2012). The ILO report also provides a focus on the EU countries hardest hit by the crisis. Between 1991 and 2013 in Spain the labour share fell from 62 to 54 per cent, with half of this fall occurring after 2009. In Greece the share decreased from 57 to 48 per cent, with a loss of 7 percentage points from 2009.

In the 2012 Employment Outlook, the OECD had investigated the falling labour share from 1990 to 2009, finding that all OECD countries – except Greece, Denmark, the Czech Republic and Iceland – experienced a fall that went in parallel with increasing income inequality. The fall is greater when we consider the business sector only, as opposed to the total economy. In one-third of OECD countries the fall was greater than 5 percentage points (OECD, 2012: 113, 117). Moreover, the OECD pointed out the polarisation that has taken place within wages. In the past two decades the 'wages' of the top 1 per cent of the income distribution have increased by 20 per cent, while labour income for poorer workers has declined. In this way, the decline of the labour share is significantly greater if we exclude the remuneration of the top 1 per cent – in the US and Canada the fall in the labour share doubles to 4.5 and 6 percentage points, respectively, and in Italy it reaches 9 percentage points (OECD, 2012: 113–15). The OECD argued that 'the worsening of the labour income share might have an adverse effect on the level of aggregate demand and on how quickly economies can recover from the recent crisis', concluding that 'these trends might endanger social cohesion' (OECD, 2012: 110).

Complementary evidence comes from the evolution of the capital share in national income. Thomas Piketty (2013: 351; see Piketty and Zucman (2014a) for the methodology), using national accounts, has documented the long-term rise of the share of capital from 1975 to 2010, reported in Figure 2.2. At the start the share ranged from 15 to 25 per cent; by 2010 countries were grouped between 25 and 30 per cent. Italy has had one of the highest values, growing until the 2008 crisis (these data probably are not adjusted for the importance of self-employment and include

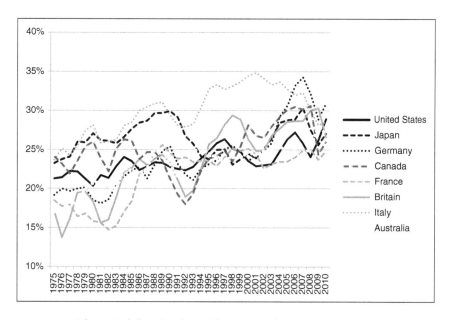

FIGURE 2.2 The capital share in advanced countries, 1975–2010

Source: From Thomas Piketty, *Capital in the XXI Century*, Cambridge, MA, Harvard University Press, 2014, Figure 6.5, p.222. For sources and data see piketty.pse.ens.fr/capital21c

the remuneration of their labour); Japan had a large share until 1990; Germany has emerged since 2006 with the highest values of the capital share. As already pointed out, the lower shares for the US and the UK result from considering most of the remuneration of top managers that mix a variety of incomes as labour income.

The period between 1975 and 1990 is the one with the most rapid growth of the capital share in income, with large increases in France, Germany and the UK. Recessions always lead to a temporary fall of the capital share, and the one in 1992 is particularly serious. By 1994, however, capital had recovered its previous share and started a major rise, supported by the full liberalisation of capital movements and the financial boom associated to the 'new economy'. The recession of 2001 interrupted again the rise of the capital share, followed by a new recovery and an overall stability. Surprisingly, the crisis of 2008 and the recession of 2009 did not lead to a generalised fall of the capital share in all countries.

The interpretation offered by Piketty (2013) is that this rise is associated to a growing capital/income ratio – resulting from an elasticity of substitution between capital and labour above one – and to a stronger 'bargaining power' of capital vs. labour in a context of greater international mobility of capital: 'it is likely that the two effects have reinforced each other in the last decades, and is possible that they will continue to do so in the future' (Piketty, 2013: 351). The transformations of the economy and the power of capital over labour are identified as key drivers of inequality.

A fundamental mechanism behind falling labour shares is the inability of wages to keep up with productivity increases. If both had moved at the same pace, the functional distribution of income would have not changed. Figure 2.3, again from the ILO report, points out the broadening gap between labour productivity and real wages in the aggregate of 36 developed economies.[2] The former is measured by GDP per worker, considering the whole economy and ignoring changes in hours worked, in the quality of employment and in capital. Wages are deflated by the consumer price index that reflects workers' standard of living (using the GDP deflator, the gap would be halved). Putting 1991 data equal to 100, productivity in 2013 has reached 117 and wages are just above 106. Again, the recession of 2009 is visible with a marked fall of GDP per worker; after 2010, however, there is a return to the previous trend of productivity increase. Conversely, after the crisis the dynamics of real wages has been basically flat. The widespread gap between the dynamics of productivity and that of wages within industries is documented also by the OECD (2012: 121).

Why have wages not been able to catch up with productivity? Outcomes in the distribution of income between capital and labour depend on the overall balance of forces in the economy and in workplaces. Several developments – including the pressure from finance for high returns in firms, international production, labour-saving technologies, the precarisation of employment, the weakening of unions and the reduced role of national labour contracts – have made it more difficult for workers to obtain wage increases in line with output per worker. In fact, ILO data

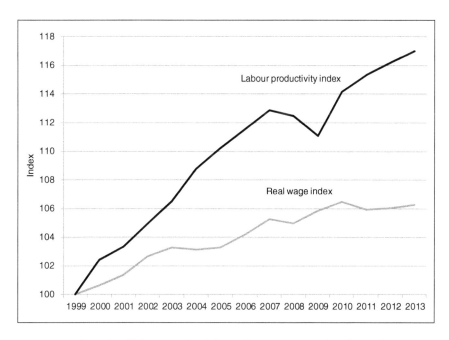

FIGURE 2.3   Growth of labour productivity and average wages in advanced countries, 1991–2013

Note: Wage growth is calculated as a weighted average of year-on-year growth in average monthly real wages in 36 economies. Index is based to 1999 because of data availability. Data from ILO Global Wage Database; ILO Trends Econometric Model.
Source: *ILO Global Wage Report* 2014–15: 8 © 2015 International Labour Organization

show that in these developed economies real wages increased by 0.1 per cent in 2012 and 0.2 per cent in 2013 (ILO, 2015: 6). Italy and the UK have been the major countries with significant losses in average real wages. Looking at the EU countries hardest hit by the crisis, putting the real average wage index equal to 100 in 2007, in 2013 Spain decreased to 97 and Greece to 76 (ILO, 2015: 7).

How do such developments in wages and profits affect inequality? Wages are the largest – and often only – source of income for most households; profits are distributed to a large extent to the richest 10 per cent of the population. For advanced economies wages represent almost 80 per cent of total household income, with higher values for the US, Germany, the UK and Sweden. Italy and Greece have a share of income from self-employment above 20 per cent; when combined with wages, all labour income is again close to 80 per cent, while old age pensions account for more than 15 per cent. This situation is common to most income groups; only the poorest 10 per cent has a majority of income coming from non-labour sources – either social transfers or pensions – with wide variation according to national specificities (ILO, 2015: 36–7).

The methodology developed by Di Nardo *et al.* (1996) allows us to explore the factors that shape a change in household inequality levels, including changes in wages, in employment (a loss of job by a family member means a loss of wage), in other incomes, in public transfers, etc. The ILO report investigates in such a way, during the years of the crisis, the sources of increased disparities between the richest 10 per cent and the poorest 10 per cent of the population in developed economies. Comparing 2006 and 2010, Spain and the US are the countries with the largest absolute increase in the P90/P10 ratio – the ratio between the income above which we find the richest 10 per cent and the one below which we find the poorest 10 per cent. In Spain the income threshold for the richest 10 per cent is now 5.7 times the income below which we find the poorest 10 per cent and was 4.4 times in 2006. In the US it is 10.6 times, and was 9.5 times in 2006. For Spain 90 per cent of this increase in inequality is the result of changes in employment and wages (job losses and wage decline for the poorest, gains for the richest), while changes in other incomes account for the rest. For the US, the combined effect of changes in jobs and wages account for 140 per cent of the variation in inequality, and other incomes have compensated to some extent such growing disparities in labour market outcomes (ILO, 2015: 30). In Europe a clear divide emerges between northern and central countries that have continued to expand employment – contributing in this way to a reduced inequality among households – and southern countries hardest hit by the crisis where job losses have been a major source of disparities. In Germany, the UK, France and Sweden new jobs have contributed to reduce disparities, while the unequal distribution of other incomes (mainly from capital) has been a major force of inequality. On the whole, Germany and the UK reported an overall modest reduction of disparities, while France and Sweden had an increase of our measure of inequality.

Such a range of data highlight the difficulty that labour has had in advanced countries in maintaining its share of national income in the face of deep changes in the organisation of the economy – rise of finance, technological change, international production – in the operation of labour markets – precarisation of employment and reduced union power – and in the context of the crisis started in 2008. The growing power of capital over labour clearly emerges as a key factor in the increase of inequality.

2.3 The problem of the very rich

A very important development of recent years in many countries is the increasing share of income accruing to the already rich. This partly overlaps with the above evidence on the rising share of capital as the richest 10 per cent, 1 per cent or even 0.1 per cent of the population concentrate income from business profits, financial rents, top management and 'star' professional activities. Crucial evidence on this problem has emerged from detailed studies based on tax records that distinguish taxpayers by income classes, reporting the number of individuals belonging to each class, mean income and its source (labour, firm, capital, rents, transfers) (Atkinson

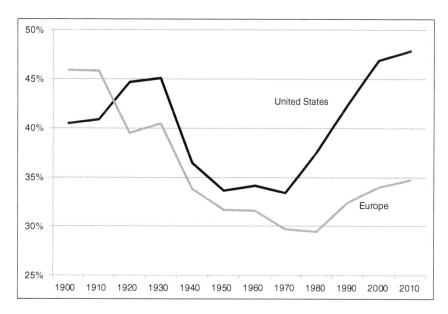

FIGURE 2.4   The share of income of the richest 10 per cent in the US and Europe, 1900–2010

Source: From Thomas Piketty, *Capital in the XXI Century*, Cambridge, MA, Harvard University Press, 2014, Figure 9.8, p.324. For sources and data see piketty.pse.ens.fr/capital21c

and Piketty, 2007, 2010; Atkinson *et al.*, 2011). Top income data refer to individual gross incomes reported to the fiscal administration (some differences exist in definition across countries). Inequality measured by these data could be reduced once taxes and transfers are paid and when we move from individual to household incomes (converted through the scales of equivalence that allow us to compare incomes of households of a different size).

The work by Atkinson, Piketty and their colleagues has highlighted in a very effective way the extreme inequalities associated to the rising incomes of the very rich. The well-known graph reported in Figure 2.4 shows the long-run evolution – from 1900 to 2010 – of the the share of income of the top 10 per cent. In the US in 2000 this share surpassed that of 1930, continuing to increase above 45 per cent. At the start of the twentieth century the US were less unequal than Europe, with its feudal tradition. The rapid industrialisation and the financial boom of the 'belle époque' from 1910 to 1930 fuelled a major rise of inequality, with the top income decile obtaining 45 per cent of total income. The Great Crash and the Great Depression reduced that share by one-quarter in 1940; the Second World War further reduced it below 35 per cent in 1950. From the 1950s to the 1970s the share of the very rich was stable or declining, constrained by a reduced role of finance and capital controls, greater power of labour in the industrial expansion and the expansion of the welfare state. In 1980, however, the rise of top incomes started, with a steep increase until 2000 and a slower one – affected by the 2008 crisis – after that.

Patterns in Europe are rather different. Piketty considers the UK, Germany, France and Sweden (that rank in this order in terms of today's inequality), and their arithmetic mean is shown in Figure 2.4. At the start of the twentieth century inequality in Europe was as high as the current one in the US; the First World War and the collapse of aristocratic élites led to a first decline between 1910 and 1920; the 'belle époque' of finance allowed a reprieve, but from the Great Crash onwards trends in Europe mirrored that of the US, with lower values resulting from the greater role of the State in the economy, the power of unionised labour and more extensive welfare reforms. The lowest share of the very rich was reached in 1980, under 30 per cent of total income. Since then, however, the rise has started in Europe too, reaching 35 per cent, and has not been stopped by the 2008 crisis.

Even within the very rich – the top 10 per cent – income is unevenly distributed, and the 'ultra rich' 1 per cent of individuals concentrate about half of the share of the top decile. A systematic analysis of national trends is possible with our calculations on the database made available by Piketty and colleagues. Figure 2.5 summarises the evidence for the US and a larger group of European countries. The shares of income of the richest 1 per cent vary widely among countries: the US and the UK are char-acterised by the highest values – between 15 and 18 per cent in 2010. Germany, Italy and France follow, while the Netherlands and Sweden have the lowest values, below 7 per cent. However, the rise since 1980 is generalised in all countries, again with the US and the UK showing the most extreme values, returning to levels typical of the

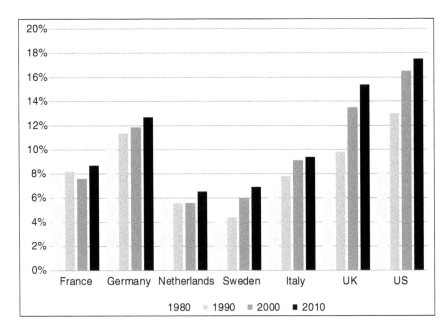

FIGURE 2.5 The top 1 per cent income share in advanced countries, 1980–2010

Source: Computations on World Top Income Database (http://topincomes.parisschoolofeconomics.eu/)

early twentieth century (if capital gains are added to incomes, the share of the 'ultra rich' in the US further increases by 3 percentage points).

We could repeat the exercise, and find that within the 'ultra rich' 1 per cent there is a top group of the 0.1 per cent – the 'incredibly rich' individuals – that control 9 per cent of total income in the US and 6 per cent in the UK, more than four times the level of the 1970s (Alvaredo *et al.*, 2013).

These data can only be interpreted as the outcome of our second 'engine of inequality'– the rise of 'oligarch capitalism'– that will be discussed later in this chapter with regard to wealth inequality, and in the following chapter with regard to inter-generational consequences.

Where do such 'incredible' incomes come from? Atkinson, Piketty and their colleagues have argued that in past decades the richest individuals mostly earned their income from capital and rents; conversely, in the last three decades the 'labour' income of the very rich appears to have increased with the extreme salaries of top managers (especially in the financial sectors) and also 'star' professionals in sport and show business (Atkinson *et al.*, 2011). Today, in the US the share of 'labour' earnings in the income of the top 0.1 per cent is about 45 per cent and has increased by 20 percentage points since the 1970s (Alvaredo *et al.*, 2013). Even in Italy the composition of top incomes has changed since the 1980s: the share of labour income (from employment and self-employment) of the top 1 per cent rose from 46 to 71 per cent and the share of capital income and rents was proportionally reduced (Alvaredo and Pisano, 2010).

Lazonick (2015: 28–31) has noted that the definition of salaries includes compensation from the realised gains on exercising stock options and the vesting of stock awards, as this stock-based pay is not reported in tax returns. Looking at the 500 highest paid executives in the US in the ExecuComp database – all members of the richest 0.1 per cent – in 2013 they had an average total compensation of $24.4 million; 84 per cent came from gains on exercising stock options and the vesting of stock awards, while salaries and bonuses accounted for just 5 per cent. A study by Bakija *et al.* (2012: 1) found that 'executives, managers, supervisors and financial professionals account for about 60% of the top 0.1% of income earners'. What emerges is that a dominant part of the income of the richest 0.1 per cent comes from stock-based pay whose value is driven by the rise of finance and by the timing of the exercise of stock options, where top managers have insider knowledge (Lazonick, 2015: 32). At the root of the extreme incomes of the 'incredibly rich' there are the booming stock markets and the rents top managers can obtain from their position of power. There is no room for explanation of this pattern based on the productivity of top managers and the role of technology.

The evidence so far has pointed out the rise of the share of the very rich in total incomes. But what has happened to other income groups? We can investigate how the threshold separating the income of the richest 10 per cent from the other 90 per cent compares with the median of the income distribution – the income threshold that divides the population in half. Figure 2.6 shows changes in the ratio between the 90th and the 50th percentile of the distribution (P90/P50) of

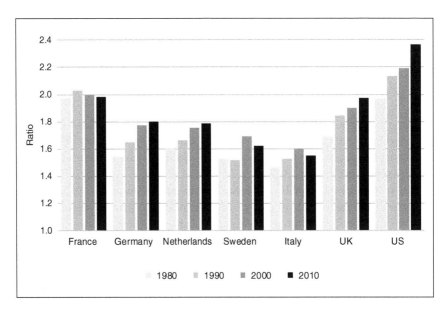

FIGURE 2.6   The P90/P50 ratio in gross earnings of employees in advanced economies, 1980–2010

Note: Ratio between the income threshold of the top 10% of incomes and the median of the income distribution.
Source: Calculations on data from the Chartbook of Economic Inequality (www.chartbookofeconomicinequality.com/)

individual earnings. It shows that in the US in 2010 the threshold identifying the top 10 per cent was 2.4 times the median US income, as opposed to less than two times in 1980. In other words the distribution of income has become more skewed towards the rich, even without considering the major rise of the incomes of the top 10 per cent; similar trends are found in the UK, Germany and the Netherlands, although at lower inequality levels. France has a high but stable ratio, while Italy and Sweden have the lowest gap between the rich and median incomes.

A similar ratio can be calculated between the income beyond which we find the richest 10 per cent and the upper limit of the poorest 10 per cent (P90/P10 ratio). Considering inequalities in labour income and comparing 1970 and 1990, the ratio has increased from 3.2 to 4.5 in the US, from 2.5 to 3.3 in the UK and has remained at 2.1 in Sweden (Piketty, 2002). The very rich, in other words, have increased their distance both from the very poor and from the middle of the income distribution.

2.4 The distribution of household income

If we want a comprehensive picture of the overall change in the distribution of income, we need to move from individual earnings (gross of taxes) to household income, where families share the different sources of incomes their members receive and an adjustment for size of families is made through equivalence scales. Market incomes are made by the gross incomes earned by all household members and come from all market sources (employment, self-employment, firms, capital and rents). We can measure inequality in the distribution of household income using the Gini coefficient, which ranges from zero (perfectly equal distribution) to one (one household concentrating all income).

The sources of these data are surveys on households where information on the different types of income is obtained; such data are made available by the OECD, the World Bank, the World Institute for Development Economics Research (WIDER), the Luxembourg Income Study and other sources.[3] However, it is well known that household surveys generally fail to record precisely the tails of the income distribution; both the very rich and the poorest (especially immigrant households) tend to be under-sampled in income surveys, resulting in an under estimation of inequality.

Household income, moreover, can be substantially lower than national income, and much closer to household final consumption; the rest is accounted for by savings by firms and by the net balances of the public sector and the balance of payments. Deaton (2005) reports that, in the US, household income is about 70 per cent of GDP and that, considering 272 surveys of households in different countries, household income on average is just 57 per cent of GDP (Deaton, 2005: 4; Anand and Segal, 2014: 947). This means that the inequality measured among households does not include all the forces that, in a national economy, may produce disparities – including the functional distribution of income, the role of the business sector, etc.

The focus of this section is on the distribution of income across households. As discussed in the introduction, we can compare inequality emerging from market outcomes (in Figure 2.7) and assess the redistributive impact of taxes and public transfers (in Figure 2.8) and of the provision of public services (in Figure 2.9).

Market income distribution among households, and its trend, depends on several factors. First, the inequality within each income source and the share of total income obtained by that source are important – for instance, the increasing share of capital income tends to increase inequality because capital income distribution is usually very unequal among households. Second, the number of household components and income recipients matters. A higher participation rate of females belonging to the poorest households reduces inequality; if females of richer households enter employment, inequality increases. Third, the income gaps among household components are relevant – when couples comprise two high earners (the so-called assortative mating) market income inequality grows.

Extensive studies have documented the general rise in income inequality in advanced countries in the last three decades (see OECD, 2008, 2011, 2015; Salverda *et al.*, 2014; Bogliacino and Maestri, 2014; Morelli *et al.*, 2014). In this section we focus on a selected group of countries – in Europe and the US – that are representative of the diversity of inequality patterns. In the period 1985–2010 disparities – measured by the Gini coefficient – have increased everywhere, with

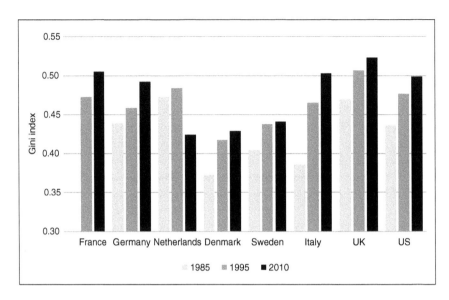

FIGURE 2.7 Gini index of inequality in household market incomes, 1985–2010

Note: Gini index on equivalised household market incomes.
Source: Calculations on the OECD database www.oecd.org/social/income-distribution-database.htm,
May 2015

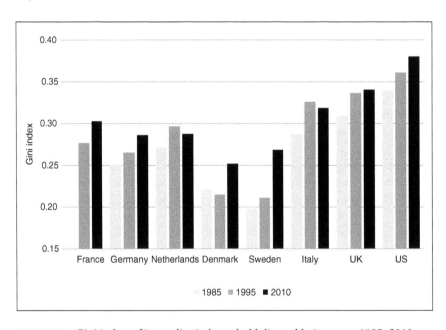

FIGURE 2.8 Gini index of inequality in household disposable incomes, 1985–2010

Note: Gini index on equivalised household disposable incomes, after taxes and monetary transfers.
Source: Calculations on the OECD database www.oecd.org/social/income-distribution-database.htm,
May 2015

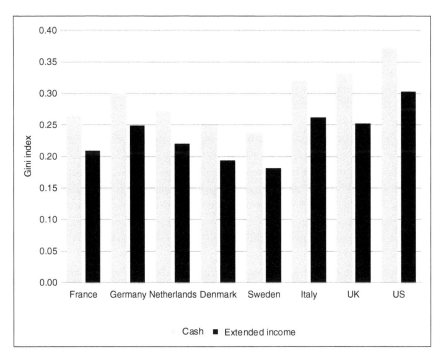

FIGURE 2.9 Gini index of inequality in cash disposable incomes and in extended income considering public services, 2007

Note: Gini index on equivalised household market incomes (after taxes and monetary transfers) and on extended income (including the value of public services obtained).
Source: Adapted from OECD (2011), data from (www.oecd.org/social/income-distribution-database.htm)

a partial exception for the Netherlands. The highest increases took place from the mid-1980s to the mid-1990s, except for Germany, where inequality has increased most in the second part of the observed period. In 2010 the UK, France, Italy, the US and Germany ranked (in this order) as the most unequal rich countries, with Gini values around 0.50, while the Netherlands, Denmark and Sweden had a lower inequality, with Gini values around 0.43.

Can policies affect such market outcomes? In Figure 2.8 we show the values of the Gini coefficients for the disposable monetary income for households – income after taxes and transfers. The redistributive impact of public action is significant, especially in Europe, with a substantial lowering of inequality levels. In 2010 the US, the UK, Italy, France, the Netherlands and Germany rank (in this order) as the most unequal countries, with Gini values ranging from 0.38 to 0.28. Since 1985, however, the same general pattern of rising inequalities is evident even after redistribution; the more equal societies – Denmark and Sweden – experienced between 1995 and 2010 the largest rise of inequality in disposable incomes of all countries. In the last period the Netherlands and Italy recorded a slight reduction in the Gini coefficient and in the UK its growth has been modest. The increase in the Gini indexes has continued in most countries when we look at the 2013 data reported by the OECD (2015: 24, Figure 1.3).

Outside these countries, Spain, Portugal and Greece had a partly different pattern, as they experienced a delayed reduction of inequality after the end of dictatorships in the 1970s, a fall that continued in some cases for several years (Bogliacino and Maestri, 2014: 16).

The average household disposable income was heavily affected by the crisis started in 2008, with a stagnation or fall in real terms in most OECD countries. In the countries most hit by the recession, the losses reached 8 per cent per year in Greece and 3.5 per cent per year in Spain, Ireland and Iceland. Behind such averages, however, the fall in disposable income was concentrated in the poorest households; in Spain the bottom 10 per cent of the distribution had a loss of almost 13 per cent per year, while the richest 10 per cent had a reduction of 1.5 per cent only (OECD, 2015: 24).

Behind the aggregate measures of inequality different drivers are at work that can be identified by the combined use of the different indicators. Several studies – including the OECD (2008) report – have pointed out that a rise in income shares by the top quintile of the income distribution (the richest 20 per cent of households) has been a key determinant of greater inequalities in most countries. In the last 20 years, the average annual growth of real incomes of the top quintile has been twice as large as the one of the bottom quintile (the poorest 20 per cent of households) (OECD, 2008). Again, this evidence is consistent – in spite of the different perspective and data sources – with the previous findings on the rising share of capital and of top incomes.

Considering the data on household disposable income – after taxes and transfers – the decrease reported for the Netherlands (Figure 2.8) has been mainly due to the increase in participation rates of females belonging to less advantaged households and has been favoured by gender reconciliation measures and the introduction of part-time contractual arrangements (Kenworthy and Pontusson, 2005).

In the case of Italy, the large increase of market income inequality from 1985 to 2010, and the reduction of disposable income inequality, have been explored by several studies. The main rise of the Gini index was associated to the effects of the 1992 recession and to the restrictive fiscal policies that were introduced (Ballarino *et al.*, 2014). Through a decomposition of the Gini index on market inequality by income sources, Fiorio *et al.* (2012) found that the main driver of divergence were labour incomes (mostly by self-employed). Over these years Italy experienced a substantial growth in employment, which – by reducing the number of zero earners – is considered the crucial driver of a decrease of inequality. Italy's employment growth did not reduce inequality, as a large part of new jobs went to females belonging to better-off households, especially in the southern regions (Ballarino *et al.*, 2014). On the other hand, new jobs have often been associated to low wages and to widening wage disparities due to labour market deregulation. The resulting rise in inequality is also affected by the increasing share of self-employment incomes, the rise in rents and returns on financial capital. Changes in these other sources of income have expanded overall disparities. The result is that, since the 1990s, substantial increases in living standards have benefitted managers, pensioners, self-employed and rentiers, while disadvantaging white-collar and blue-collar workers (Brandolini, 2005). True inequality could also be higher because of unreported income and tax evasion, which mainly advantages those on the upper part of the income distribution.

In the case of the US, a useful summary of these dynamics is provided by Atkinson and Bourguignon (2014b: xix, xx) with graphs mapping the Gini coefficient for household gross income and the share of the top 0.1 per cent in gross income; both variables show a strong increase starting in the early 1980s after a long period of stability. However, the earnings of the top decile measured as a percentage of median income have had a continuing rise since 1945, from less than 150 per cent to close to 250 per cent, suggesting that the 'distancing of the top' has been a permanent aspect of US income distribution. From 1945 to 1980 such a pattern, however, was compensated by a 'catching up of the bottom', documented by the rapid fall over that period of the share of the US population living below the official poverty line – fallen from 35 per cent in 1950 to just above 10 per cent at the end of the 1970s. From the 1980s growth at the top continued and improvement at the bottom stopped, leading to the change of direction of the Gini coefficient, which started a steady rise.

Finally, a thorough assessment of the redistributive role of the State should include not just taxes and monetary transfers, but also the activities that provide services outside the market – such as health, education and caring – offered to all citizens in particular social conditions as part of their social rights. This State provision limits the range of economic activities based on ability to pay and introduces the principle that in some fields of crucial social relevance services should be granted to all and funded through general taxation. This was a fundamental principle of the expansion of the welfare state in post-war decades – when inequality had the steepest fall – and plays a key role in assuring the basic conditions for the development of individuals' capabilities and for their equality of opportunities.

How can we account for the impact of these activities on inequality? Non-market public services granted to all as citizenship rights have a pervasive egalitarian effect in economic, social and political contexts that may, however, be difficult to quantify. The simplest way to proceed is to consider them 'transfers in kind' that integrate monetary transfers by the State. We could assign to all individuals a share of the cost of such services as the monetary equivalent of the services they have obtained. If we compare the same service provided free by the State and at a price by private organisations, it makes sense to consider that all users of the former have had an additional consumption (paid through taxes) that avoided the expenditure sustained by the buyers of the latter. In this case, we can add to individual (or household) incomes the relevant share of the monetary cost of the services they have obtained, and recalculate inequality on this disposable income adjusted for public services.

Limitations in the availability of recent data and methodological problems are obstacles to such a thorough assessment. The more systematic study available is in the OECD report 'Divided We Stand' (OECD, 2011: chapter 8), where a wide range of public services are considered – health, education, childhood services, services to the elderly, social housing and other services (to the disabled, unemployed, etc). Such public provision is of great relevance, accounting – when the value of services is calculated at their cost of production – for 20 per cent of GDP in Denmark and Sweden and 12–13 per cent in Italy and the US. Education and health are the most important components everywhere, accounting for more than three-quarters of all public provisions. More importantly, the provision of public services outside the market is more important than cash transfers from the State to households in almost all countries (Italy is an exception); typically, the former are one-third higher than the latter. Looking at the impact of public services on households we find even higher effects. When we add the monetary value of services to disposable income – post-tax and transfers – we find an increase in average household income close to 40 per cent in Denmark and Sweden and of 29 per cent in the OECD average. This increase is relevant for all households, but in percentage of disposable income is of vital relevance for the poorer ones. The rise in income amounts to 76 per cent for the poorest 20 per cent of households and to 14 per cent for the richest quintile (OECD, 2011: 314–16, Table 8.1).

By offering a generally egalitarian set of public services – some of which are in fact targeted to the poor – State policies can indeed significantly reduce the inequality that we have measured so far in monetary terms. Figure 2.9 reports the OECD data for the countries we have considered, comparing for 2007 the value of the Gini index calculated on household 'cash' disposable income (after taxes and transfers) and the Gini index on the 'extended' income that includes the imputed value of public services. The provision of public services leads to a general reduction of inequalities in all countries and to some changes in the rankings. In percentage terms, the Gini on 'extended' income falls by 17–19 per cent in Germany, the US, Italy and the Netherlands, and by 21–24 per cent in France, Sweden, Denmark and the UK. The US remains the most unequal country. In the UK the extent of provision of public services brings inequality below the Gini index for Italy and close to the value for Germany. The Netherlands has less redistribution than France, while Denmark and Sweden emerge again as the most egalitarian countries, with a significantly reduced Gini index below 0.20.

When we compare data for 2007 with data for 2000 divergent trends emerge. In France and Sweden we find that disparities in 'cash' disposable income have fallen, also bringing down inequality in 'extended' income; in all other countries we consider (and the OECD-17 average) both measures in 2007 are higher than in 2000. All countries except the UK have experienced a reduction in the redistributive impact of public services (measured as a percentage of 'cash' disposable income), suggesting that cuts in public services have reduced their egalitarian effect. In fact, the OECD report shows that the greater the fall in the share of public services in household disposable income – associated to cuts in expenditures – the deeper the fall in their contribution to reducing 'cash' inequalities (OECD, 2011: 330–1,

Table 8.8, Figure 8.11). Since 2007, the impact of the crisis and of austerity policies in most countries has further reduced the redistributive effect of public services (see Bogliacino and Maestri, 2014: 23).

The different measures of inequality discussed above have recorded a substantial increase of disparities between the 1980s and today in all advanced countries. The rise has sometimes been steady, in other cases it has been concentrated in a period and followed by stability. Across countries different factors have played a key role – the share of income going to capital, or the income of the richest 10 per cent, the distance between top and median incomes, or between median and bottom incomes – and the relevance of policy has differed, with a different ability of taxes, transfers and the provision of public services to reduce the disparity of the distribution emerging from market earnings.

2.5 Inequality within labour income

The third 'engine of inequality' we identified in chapter 1 is the 'individualisation' of economic and social conditions. This means that disparities have increased within types of income and within social groups, variously defined. Much attention has been devoted to the growing inequalities within labour incomes, resulting from the rapid rise of top incomes and the stagnation or fall of lower wages. We have already documented the former and pointed out that the remuneration of top managers and professionals – mostly made of stock-based pay – can hardly be considered a 'wage'. Disparities within wages, however, have greatly increased at all levels.

A recent Eurofound study (2015a) examined wage inequality (for full-time equivalent wages in purchase power parities (PPPs)) considering Europe as a whole and found an overall Gini coefficient in 2011 of 0.346. Wage disparities within Europe declined up to 2008 as a result of the convergence in average wages of central-eastern European countries, while in southern Europe no real increase took place, and German wages stagnated. Since 2008 the crisis has led to a rising inequality driven by disparities within countries, with major wage decreases in southern Europe. Comparing countries and industries, a major role of collective bargaining emerges, leading to higher and more equal wages (Eurofound, 2015a: 61–2). Moreover, the rise in 'non-standard' forms of employment – temporary and precarious work, outsourced self-employment jobs, etc. – has been identified as major factor in rising inequality, reflecting the changing balance of forces between capital and labour (ILO, 2015; OECD, 2015).

Mainstream interpretations of disparities within wages have argued that this is largely because of differences in skills and education; the argument is that market outcomes reflect individual differences in education, abilities and effort, and that such disparities are the result of 'merit' that deserves to be rewarded by labour market outcomes. A large literature – recently surveyed by Salverda and Checchi (2014) – has addressed such questions, arguing that disparities within wages are indeed a key determinant of the overall rise in income inequalities. A first stream of studies has investigated the impact on wage inequality of the shifts in the demand

and supply of labour resulting from changes in education, technology, globalisation, etc. A second stream of research has considered the impact on earning inequality of labour market institutions – such as minimum wage, union presence, employment protection and unemployment benefits.

What is the empirical evidence of the ability of education to explain the growth of earnings inequality? Mainstream views, largely based on studies in the US and the UK, have argued that growing inequality since the 1980s has been driven by the increasing skill premium for high-skilled workers (Bound and Johnson, 1992; Katz and Murphy, 1992). Skill biased technological change (SBTC, that is complementary to higher skills) and globalisation (that replaces low-skilled workers in advanced countries with the increasing supply of workers in developing countries) have been considered as the most important causes of the rise in the skill premium. In this view, differences in human capital are a key driver of wage inequality and investment in higher education is generally recommended as the best policy for both productivity growth and for reducing inequality.

However, detailed empirical studies suggest that human capital variables, such as experience and education, are able to explain at most a third of the variance in wages, while residual or within-group wage inequality – i.e. wage dispersion among workers with the same education – represents the largest part of this variance (Lemieux, 2006). In other terms, while differently educated individuals experience wage gaps, wage disparities are also found between individuals with the same education (e.g. inequality within groups with the same education).

We report here results from the study by Franzini and Raitano (forthcoming) on European countries, using data from the EU Statistics on Income and Living Conditions (EU-SILC) survey of households (Figure 2.10). Workers are divided into three subgroups according to their educational attainments, and disparities in wages are associated either to differences in skills ('between-group inequality') or to factors not related to skills ('within-group inequality'). The index used is the mean logarithmic deviation because it is perfectly decomposable among subgroups – i.e. can be expressed as the sum of between and within inequality.[4] The decomposition by the three educational groups shows that in EU15 countries educational attainments explain a very small share of wage disparities – 12.5 per cent of total earnings inequality in France, 12 per cent in the UK, 10 per cent in Italy, as low as 3.2 per cent in Sweden – as shown in Figure 2.10. Around 90 per cent of the wage gap among workers is linked to within-group inequality, i.e. to differences not directly related to education degrees (similar results are in Cholezas and Tsakloglou, 2007).

The time trend of within-group inequality has been investigated for Italy by Franzini and Raitano (2014), using a long panel dataset tracking private employees. Considering weekly wages of full-time workers, results show that the share of inequality due to educational attainments has constantly fallen since 1992; the share due to the between group component decreased from 16.5 per cent in 1992 to 8.9 per cent in 2007.

This empirical evidence suggests that other determinants – different from education – are affecting the rising disparities in labour earnings. The growing

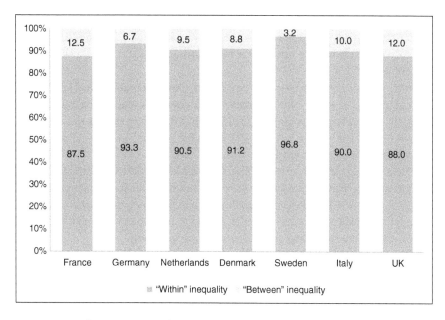

FIGURE 2.10   The importance of educational levels on inequality in gross earnings, 2006

Note: Individuals are grouped in three educational groups; inequality is measured by the mean logarithmic deviation, decomposed between the (small) share due to disparities between educational groups and the (large) share due to disparities within each educational group.
Source: Franzini and Raitano (forthcoming), data from EU-SILC survey (2007)

power of capital over labour and the individualisation of economic conditions – two of our 'engines of inequality' – can highlight much of the developments leading to higher inequality among wages. The labour force has become more segmented on the basis of ethnic or migrant status and on the basis of the labour contract in force, with the diffusion of precarious employment and of different contracts for the same job. Union power has been reduced, with a lower union membership, militancy and ability to protect working conditions especially for the weakest groups of workers. The coverage of national collective contracts has been reduced, wage setting at the company level has expanded and minimum wages have not been effective in protecting low earners. Employment protection legislation has been scaled back in most countries, leaving more room for disparities in wages (see Salverda and Checchi, 2014: 1, 631). Some of these issues will be addressed in chapter 4, looking for explanations of the current rise in inequality.

2.6 Inequalities at the regional and world level

The analysis so far has focused on inequalities within countries. There are many reasons for the relevance of such a perspective. People assess their wellbeing in the context of the society where they live, and inequalities within their countries are those that matter most. National economies are the units where governments can introduce policies that affect inequality through taxation, transfers and public services, and most data we can use for investigating inequality are available at the national level.

Other perspectives, however, may be relevant. One is the subnational level, looking at disparities at the levels of regions within countries, and within Europe as a whole. The other one is the global level, looking at disparities among all the world's citizens.

First, when we look at disparities within the regions of a country, we may find novel results. As pointed out by Bogliacino and Maestri (2014: 22), in the case of Italy inequality within regions tends to be low, but the diversity of incomes among regions leads to the high level of overall inequality documented for the country as a whole. National patterns may therefore be the result of more complex dynamics, with some regions increasing and others reducing inequality.

Second, we can consider inequalities in Europe as a whole. The previous analysis has found that individual European countries have lower disparities than the US. When we consider the EU as a whole, however, intra-European disparities in individual incomes appear to be greater than those in the US (Galbraith, 2012). Meliciani (2015) has investigated disparities among the regions of the European Union, finding that there is weak evidence of convergence in GDP per capita and an increase in disparities in employment rates. In particular, the fall in dispersion of GDP per capita among all EU27 regions hides an increase in disparities among the regions of 'old' member states – especially after the 2008 crisis – and a catching up towards the EU average GDP per capita of some regions of 'new' central-eastern European member states, where within-country regional disparities increase. The same pattern is found also for labour productivity and employment rates.

Finally, we need to consider inequalities at the global level. Economic inequality at the international level has been explored on the basis of three types of measures: differences between national per capita incomes; inequality between country averages weighted by population; and inequality among all the world's individuals (Milanovic, 2005). Over the past century – considering Gini coefficients – there is a clear increase in the first definition of inequality, an increase followed by a moderate reduction since the 1960s in the second one, and an increase followed by a stability since the 1960s in the third one (Milanovic, 2005: 143).

The latter measure – inequality among all world individuals – is the most important indicator, although it poses several methodological problems – comparability of sources, use of household surveys, national accounts or tax return data, conversion of currencies using purchasing power parities, choice of equivalence scales, etc. – and the adopted solution may influence results.

Recent works by Milanovic (2012), Lakner and Milanovic (2013) and Anand and Segal (2014) have explored this issue. Milanovic (2012) has provided new data – based on household surveys – on global income inequality on the period 1988–2005, including most world countries (103 to 124 countries) and covering almost all world GDP (95 per cent to 98 per cent of global GDP in PPP$) and world population (87 per cent to 92 per cent). Anand and Segal (2014: 953) supplement it with tax return data for the income of the top 1 per cent, as top incomes are generally excluded from survey data. They focus on the household per capita income of individuals and find that global inequalities have increased over all the period. Between 1988 and 2005 the income share of the world's richest 10 per cent increased from 58.5 to 60 per cent; the share of the richest 1 per cent went from 17.3 to 20.7 per cent; the Gini index went from 0.726 in 1988 to 0.735 in 2002 and to 0.727 in 2005; and the mean logarithmic deviation and the Theil T have also increased over the same period. It should be pointed out that in 2005 the richest 1 per cent of the world population was made by about 60 million people who have a per capita household income greater than $42,000 (the lower threshold for this group, in purchasing power parities). In the US the threshold for entering the richest 1 per cent is about twice the one at the world level. The average income of the world's richest 1 per cent is about $90,000, almost 21 times the world average, and 214 times the average of the 1.4 billion people who live below the income threshold of $1.25-a-day (in PPPs) and who account for 21 per cent of the world population (Anand and Segal, 2014: 955, 975, Table 11.3).

When the incomes of the top 1 per cent are not considered – as in Milanovic (2012), Lakner and Milanovic (2013), and in separate estimates by Anand and Segal (2014) – global inequality remains stable between 1988 and 2005. At the global level, as in advanced countries, the rise in inequality is mainly driven by the growth of top incomes.

Over this period the world distribution of income has been deeply affected by the rise of average incomes in emerging countries – most notably in China – and by the increase of domestic inequalities in both advanced and emerging countries. The decomposition of inequality measures provided by Anand and Segal (2014: Table 11.3) shows that at the global level between-country inequality still accounts for two-thirds to three-quarters of all disparities and that its reduction has been 6–8 percentage points (depending on the index used). Conversely, within-country inequality increased substantially. Given these patterns, if all between-country disparities were eliminated (i.e. all countries had the same average income), total world inequality would still be high, with a Gini index of 0.43, similar to the inequality level of China in 2005 (Anand and Segal, 2014: 963).

Still, not all emerging countries are following the same route of expanding domestic inequality. There is now strong empirical evidence that in the last decade the change of policy in most Latin American countries has led to a substantial reduction of inequality, with redistributive public policies playing a major role in this outcome (Birdsall *et al.*, 2011; Cornia, 2012).

2.7 Inequalities in wealth

We have so far investigated the annual *flows* of incomes to individuals and households. Their economic strength and wellbeing, however, are deeply affected by the *stock* of wealth they own. Piketty (2013) has shown how important wealth is for understanding the dynamics of inequality, and how complex the relationships to income growth and inequality are.

Wealth is made of real estate assets – most notably the house where a family lives – and of financial assets minus debt. Data sources are limited and difficult to compare, and include the United Nations University WIDER project, the Global Wealth Report of Credit Suisse, the Luxemburg Wealth Study and the Household Finance and Consumption Network of the European Central Bank. The main studies on wealth inequality include OECD (2008, 2015), ECB (2013), Piketty (2013), Piketty and Zucman (2014b), Maestri *et al.* (2014).

The European Central Bank (ECB, 2013) has published the first results of the survey produced by the Eurosystem Household Finance and Consumption Network with data on assets, debt, net wealth, income and consumption in 15 Eurozone countries for 2010. It provides data on *real wealth* – including the value of the main residence, other real estate property, vehicles, valuables and self-employment businesses – on *financial wealth* – including deposits, private pensions or life insurances, mutual funds, shares, bonds and other financial assets – and on household *debt* (that is subtracted from the former in order to obtain net wealth). Wealth data are not equivalised for household size (as is done for incomes), do not include the value of public pensions and in some countries private debt is highly affected by the debt incurred for undertaking higher education.

The most stinking finding is that the bottom 20 per cent of Europeans have a net wealth of zero – more precisely, the mean value of the lowest quintile is -2,800 euros; one European in five either has no assets, or his debt is higher than assets. Moving up, the second quintile has an average net wealth of €29,400, the third one €111,900, the fourth one €235,100 and the richest 20 per cent of Europeans have a mean value of €780,700 in net wealth; they own 68 per cent of total wealth. Even within this group wealth is highly concentrated, with the top 5 per cent of households owning 37.2 per cent of net wealth. Variations across countries are significant and are mainly due to the importance of home ownership; the mean net wealth of households is higher in Spain (€291,000), Italy (€275,000), Austria (€265,000) and France (€233,000), and lower in Germany (€195,000), the Netherlands (€170,000) and Finland (€161,000) (ECB, 2013:72–6, Table 4.1).

In the aggregate of 15 countries, real assets account for almost 85 per cent of total assets (gross of debt); the median value for households is €145,000. Within real assets the main residence accounts for 61 per cent, other real estate for 23 per cent and self-employed businesses for 12 per cent. In the Eurozone 60 per cent of households own the house where they live (one-third with a mortgage) and the median value of the main residence is €180,300. Considering other real assets, the median value of other real estate property is €103,000, of vehicles €7,000, of valuables €3,400 and of self-employed businesses €30,000 (ECB, 2013: 5, 27, Table 2.2).

Looking at financial assets – accounting for just 15 per cent of total assets – their composition includes 43 per cent of deposits, 26 per cent of private pensions, 9 per cent of mutual funds, 8 per cent of shares, 7 per cent of bonds and 5.3 per cent of other financial assets. The median value of financial assets for Eurozone households is €11,400, suggesting a very limited relevance of finance in the wealth of most Europeans, well below the importance found in the US and the UK. While 96 per cent of households have bank deposits, only 33 per cent have private pensions or life insurances and all the other financial assets are owned by less than 15 per cent of households. Conversely, 44 per cent of Eurozone households have debt, 23.1 per cent have mortgage debt and 29.3 per cent have other types of debt (ECB, 2013: 5).

How did the concentration of wealth change in past decades? Maestri *et al.* (2014: 88, 95, Figures 4.1, 4.3) show that a clear pattern of rising wealth inequality can be found between 1970 and 2011, and in particular in the last decade, in almost all advanced countries. As a measure we can again use the Gini coefficient, noting that it may not be directly comparable with the one calculated on incomes as the poorest deciles have negative wealth, and therefore the range of variation is no longer between zero and one. In 2011 the US show again the highest values of the Gini coefficient on wealth, above 0.8, with Denmark, Sweden and the Netherlands reaching similar levels in 2011, after rapid increases in inequality in the last decade. Germany is also rising, with a Gini coefficient around 7.5, while the UK and Italy in 2011 are below the 0.7 level as a result of a fall in recent years. The speculative bubbles of past decades have heavily affected the price dynamics of real estate and financial assets; as the 2007 crisis has led to (temporary) falls in housing and stock prices, a stabilisation or a reduction of wealth inequalities has appeared in some countries.

Wealth inequality has worsened in Nordic countries in particular. Net wealth has become negative for the four bottom wealth deciles in Denmark, for the three bottom deciles in Sweden and is negative or zero for the three bottom deciles in the Netherlands. The spread of debt is a major source of such developments, including housing and student loans. In the Netherlands, even before the crisis, housing loans were 110 per cent of the value of assets; in Sweden 25 per cent of households have a student loan (Maestri *et al.*, 2014: 91–2). However, in Nordic countries the extent of public transfers and service provision, including social housing – documented in the previous sections of this chapter – makes sure that most of the households holding no net wealth can avoid conditions of poverty.

Wealth inequality is much higher than income inequality – looking at Gini coefficients, disparities are generally twice as high – but their relationship is complex. Maestri *et al.* (2014: 98, Figure 4.7) provide a useful picture of the combinations of income and wealth disparities that are found in advanced countries, resulting from economic and institutional differences. The US, Australia and, to a lesser extent, the UK, show high inequality in both aspects. Southern European countries – Italy and Spain, but also Japan – have high disparities in income, but lower ones in wealth, mainly due to the relevance of home ownership. Conversely, Sweden, Denmark and, to a lesser extent, France, have low income inequality, resulting from an important role of the State in redistribution and public provision, but high wealth disparities.

A complementary picture of wealth dynamics is the one provided by Piketty (2013) based on tax returns – from inheritance and incomes – focusing on the evolution of top incomes in the long term. Figure 2.11 compares, over two centuries, the shares of the wealthiest 10 per cent and 1 per cent in the US and Europe – calculated as the average value for Britain, France and Sweden. From 1810 to 1910 Europe's aristocracy had an almost total control of wealth: the top 10 per cent had 80–90 per cent of wealth; the top 1 per cent had 50–65 per cent of wealth, both with a rising trend. In the US the top groups started from a much lower level, but increased their share of wealth more rapidly: the top 10 per cent went from less than 60 per cent to more than 80 per cent of total wealth; the top 1 per cent from 25–45 per cent. The two world wars brought about a steep fall of all shares; since 1950 the shares of the wealthiest Americans stabilised and rose again after 1970; in Europe the fall of both shares continued until 1970 as a result of the taxation and redistributive policies of the welfare state, rising again after 1980. In this perspective, in the US the wealthiest 10 per cent had, in 2010, more than 70 per cent of total wealth, close to the level of 1930; in Europe their share was above 60 per cent. Looking at the top 1 per cent, in 2010 their share in the US was close to 35 per cent, slightly lower than in 1930; in Europe their share of total wealth was under 25 per cent.

These data confirm that today wealth inequality is at extremely high levels and growing. In the US the concentration of wealth is particularly striking; in fact, both income and wealth inequality today are similar to the levels recorded around 1930. In Europe – where financial wealth is less important and home ownership more widely diffused – absolute levels of inequality are lower, but still at unprecedented

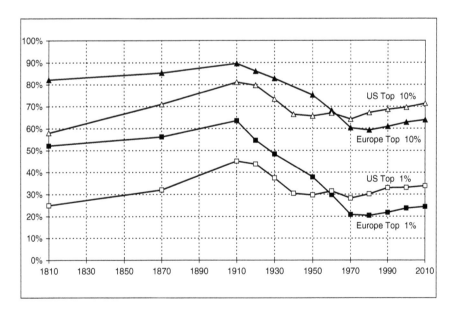

FIGURE 2.11 Wealth inequality in the US and Europe, 1810–2010: shares of the top 10 per cent and top 1 per cent

Source: from Piketty (2014) *Capital in the XXI Century*, Cambridge, MA, Harvard University Press, Figure 10.6, p. 349. For sources and data see piketty.pse.ens.fr/capital21c

levels since 1970 (Piketty, 2013: 550–7). In the analysis of Piketty, the roots of such dynamics are in the diverging patterns of the rate of return to capital and of the rate of growth of the economy – an issue that will be discussed in chapter 4, where the explanations of inequality are addressed.

The difference between the US and Europe is related to the diversity in wealth structures; in Europe two-thirds of assets are housing, and one-third is other domestic capital – businesses and financial assets – while in the US the latter account for about 60 per cent of all assets; both agricultural land and net foreign assets account for negligible shares (Piketty and Zucman, 2014b: 1, 311–14). The post-war decades have seen the diffusion of home ownership in Europe; in recent years the rising house prices have inflated such asset values, resulting in a lower concentration of wealth. In the US since the 1970s the importance of finance and the extreme rise in values associated to successive speculative bubbles have been a key driver of the country's wealth. In this regard, the rise of finance in the US has been a specific form taken by the first 'engine of inequality' discussed in chapter 1 – large and growing disparities in wealth are both the result of and a factor contributing to the power of capital over labour.

The extreme concentration of wealth now reached in the US raises new problems in terms of its inter-generational transmission through inheritance, a process that drastically reduces the possibility to acquire wealth through labour income, leading to what we have called 'oligarch capitalism' – the second 'engine of inequality' – an issue that will be addressed in the next chapter. Chapter 4 will then explore the explanations for the rising disparities we have documented in income and wealth.

Notes

1 The G20 includes Argentina, Australia, Brazil, Canada, China, France, Germany, India, Indonesia, Italy, Japan, the Republic of Korea, Mexico, the Russian Federation, Saudi Arabia, South Africa, Turkey, the UK, the US and the European Union.

2 Economies included are EU countries, the US, Canada, Norway, Iceland, Israel, Australia and New Zealand. The gap between productivity and wage growth has been documented for the US by Fleck et al. (2011) and by the Economic Report of the President (USCEA, 2014).

3 Data for individuals are transformed into the household data used here using equivalence scales. If we compare a household with one person and a household with two persons having the same total monetary income, the benefits obtained by each individual of the latter household are more than half that of the former. Market incomes are gross of taxes and public transfers. In Figure 2.8 disposable income is examined, including taxes and transfers; following standard methodology, home production, imputed rents for owner occupiers or fringe benefits are not included in disposable income.

4 Between-group inequality measures the inequality that would emerge if all individuals in a subgroup earned the mean income of the subgroup; within-group inequality is the weighted average of the inequality measured inside all subgroups.

3
FAMILY MATTERS

3.1 Introduction

The second engine of inequality we identified in chapter 1 is the structural transformation of the economic system as a result of the unprecedented importance
of top incomes, the ever stronger concentration of wealth and mechanisms that
reproduce inequality from one generation to the next through the importance of
family, heritage and lack of social mobility. 'Oligarch capitalism' is what is emerging
in advanced countries, and it resembles closely the economic and social situation
of the early twentieth century. Pointing out the importance of inherited wealth
for individual life prospects and its impact on the concentration of wealth, Piketty
(2013: 184) compared our societies to the ones described in the novels of Jane
Austen and Honoré de Balzac, where 'the past tends to devour the future' (Piketty,
2013: 600).

In this chapter we investigate two main drivers of oligarch capitalism – the
importance of inherited wealth and the influence of parents' condition on children's economic success in the labour market, two instances where 'family matters'.

3.2 Inherited wealth

Inherited wealth is a key factor in shaping economic and social inequality, and
Piketty's book (2013) shed new light on this largely neglected issue. In the period
following the Second World War, inherited wealth became less important and the
chances were high that savings out of the labour income earned during a lifetime
could lead to the accumulation of an amount of wealth comparable to the average
inherited wealth. In France, the country for which reliable data are available over
a very long period of time, according to Piketty's calculations, between 1950 and
2010 the share of annual inheritance flow over national income has gone up from a

little more than 4 per cent in 1950 to more than 12 per cent. This ratio reached its highest value (24 per cent) at the beginning of the twentieth century (Piketty, 2013: 633, Graph 11.6). In parallel, while in 1970 the share of inherited wealth in total wealth was 45 per cent, today it is close to 70 per cent, and it may stabilise at a share of 80 or 90 per cent, at a similar level to that at the start of the twentieth century (Piketty, 2013: 638, Graph 11.7; see also Piketty and Zucman, 2014b).

The growing importance of inherited wealth has many worrying implications. The past will matter more than the present and the future, thereby shaping a pattern of distribution that has little to do with merit, economic efficiency and social justice. The gap between those who live on inherited wealth and those who live on their labour earnings widens and this role of inheritance further increases income inequality. Inherited wealth is very unevenly distributed and if it gets more importance, it will translate into greater income inequality and persist across generations.

The forces behind such tendencies are easy to identify. The first one is the rise in the rate of return on wealth pointed out by Piketty's book, which has allowed an expansion of asset values transmitted through heritage.

The second force is the fiscal treatment: inheritance taxes can be an effective tool against the concentration of wealth (Bertocchi, 2007). In many countries policies have offered a more favourable fiscal treatment to inheritance, and this is a major reason for the trends we are observing. According to the recent *Worldwide Estate and Inheritance Tax Guide* by Ernst & Young (EY 2014), since 2000 several countries have cancelled their inheritance taxes, including Austria, Norway and Sweden; others took a similar step 30 years before (Australia and Canada) or simply do not have such a tax (Russia). Several other countries have introduced changes that made it much easier to transfer wealth from parents to sons, daughters or other relatives; in particular, tax rates have been reduced or exemption thresholds have been raised.

The effects on inheritance of these changes can be important. First, for a given amount of gross wealth, a greater net wealth is transferred across generations. Second, there is a greater incentive to accumulate wealth with the motivation to 'leave more' to sons (see Jappelli *et al.*, 2010 for the case of Italy).

Restoring taxes on inheritance seems necessary in order to avoid that inequality may keep increasing and, above all, that it results in undeserved privileges. The policy proposals in this regard are discussed in chapter 5.

3.3 Family background and labour income

Beside inherited wealth, family matters because it affects in more subtle ways the economic success of the new generation, in particular the income earned in the labour market. Available data show that, at least in some countries, the correlation between individuals' labour earnings and their parents' income is very high. This means that rich parents transmit to their children not only the wealth from which they will earn capital income, but also some other advantage that allows them to get, on average, a higher labour income, either as an employee or self-employed. The countries where the transmission of this advantage seems to be stronger are European Mediterranean countries, the UK and the US. One can notice that those are also countries where current income inequality is comparatively high and there are good reasons to believe that coincidence is not accidental. Indeed, one of the possible consequences of high inequality, though a neglected one, is its likely impact on the intensity of the inter-generational transmission of advantages and disadvantages, i.e. on social and economic mobility across generations. Ermisch *et al.* (2012: 3) in their introductory essay to a volume on how parents can influence the economic and social future of their children, write: 'Of all the potential consequences of rising economic inequality, none is more worrisome, or more difficult to study, than the possibility that rising inequality will have the long-term effect of reducing equality of opportunity and inter-generational mobility'.

In this chapter we provide evidence on the influence of family background on labour income in various countries, and on the correlation between the inter-generational transmission of inequality and current economic inequality. We also try to identify the channels through which such influence is exerted and their implications for policy intervention. Finally, we argue that the importance of economic and social mobility should not be underestimated: a truly democratic society cannot do without it, as emphasised by many thinkers of various credence and, in particular, of liberal conviction – from Tocqueville to Stuart Mill to Pareto. Social mobility can indeed be seen as a hallmark of modernity.

The transmission of inequality from one generation to the next has much to do with the concept of mobility. Economic and social mobility across generations can be differently interpreted and there is often some confusion in the use of these terms. Sociologists, who have studied social mobility for several decades now, usually distinguish between absolute and relative mobility (Erikson and Goldthorpe, 1992). Absolute mobility implies that the economic or social situation of children is (in some meaningful sense) better than their parents'. Relative mobility, instead, is defined as a situation in which children's places in the social and economic ranking of their generation changes compared with that of their parents a generation earlier.

This concept of mobility has much to do with inequality and its transmission from one generation to the next. In fact, if inequality is completely transmitted from parents to children, children will rank in the same order as their parents in the social or economic scale. High relative mobility means that the sons of the poor will not be concentrated at the bottom of the social scale, nor the children of the rich mainly in the upper positions. If, on the contrary, it is possible to predict precisely the position that children will have in the income distribution on the basis of their parents' position, then we can conclude that economic mobility is absent.

These positions can refer to social status or occupation (what sociologists are most interested in) or to economic conditions, as measured by income (what mainly draws economists' attention).

Social and economic mobilty are related, because social status and income are related. Generally, more prestigious social occupations bring higher income.

Here we are concerned with income and will refer to countries where the data for comparing the labour income of parents and sons/daughters are available.

The inter-generational transmission of inequality is a complex phenomenon. In its assessment there are several problems, including the availability of reliable data, the stage of the son's/daughter's career at which income should be measured, how to treat the case of children who have multiple parents and so on (Jäntti and Jenkins, 2014). A further obstacle relates to the indicator to be used for representing the degree of inter-generational transmission of inequality. It is now common practice to use the so-called inter-generational elasticity coefficient (β).[1] The closer this coefficient is to one, the stronger the transmission of inequality. When β is zero, mobility is perfect and no inequality is transmitted across generations. When it is equal to one, inequality among the offspring is a perfect mirror of that among their parents; that is, the society is completely immobile.

According to many empirical studies[2] the European countries where the β coefficient is lowest are the Nordic ones followed by Germany, Spain and France. The UK and Italy show much higher values and are the least mobile; at least 50 per cent of the inequality existing between parents is transmitted to the next generation. If we extend the analysis beyond Europe, the US emerges as an immobile society, not much different, according to this measure, from the worst-performing European countries. This finding came as a surprise to those who believed in the 'American dream' of high mobility. Canada and Australia perform much better, and even in Japan the transmission of inequality is much lower than in the US. Figure 3.1 shows these findings.

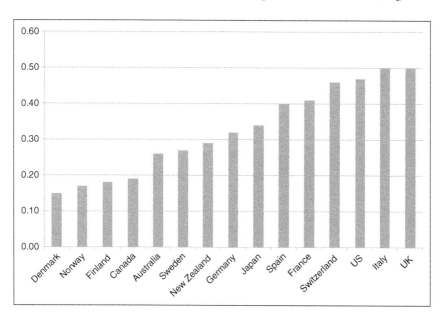

FIGURE 3.1 The transmission of inequality across generations

Note: β coefficient of inter-generational elasticity; with a value of 1, inequality among the new generation is exactly the same as in the old generation; with a value of 0 there is perfect social mobility.
Source: Corak (2013)

Is is interesting to notice that the β coefficient is not constant across deciles; in other words, it changes as we move from lower to higher levels of income. In particular, in most countries it is higher for higher-income brackets, meaning that the sons of the rich are the least mobile – i.e. have very low chances of sliding downward in the economic and social ranking with respect to their family of origin.

According to a number of empirical studies, current inequality is positively correlated with its inter-generational transmission. As Figure 3.2 shows, the countries where income inequality is low are generally countries where economic mobility is relatively high and vice versa. Italy, the UK and the US exhibit the worst performance in both these dimensions. This relationship has been labelled 'the Great Gatsby curve' by Alan Krueger (2012), then Chairman of the Council of Economic Advisors to the US President.

This is enough to challenge the idea that current inequality and its inter-generational transmission are independent phenomena, with different mechanisms at their roots. Such independence is, for instance, presumed by those who claim that equality of opportunity (usually a pre-condition for economic mobility) can be achieved independently of prior action to moderate existing inequality. The correlation suggests that income inequality could be one of the main forces behind low economic mobility. Before arriving at this conclusion, however, we must inquire into the possible mechanisms of economic immobility, assess their empirical relevance and identify the ways in which current inequality can fuel one or another of those mechanisms.

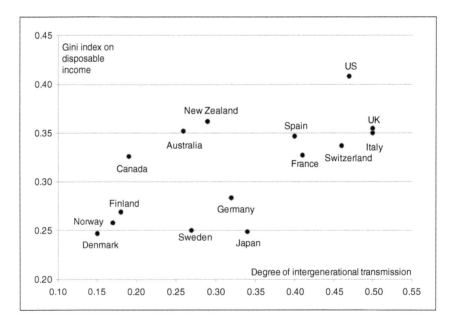

FIGURE 3.2 Inequality in disposable income and degree of inter-generational transmission

Note: β coefficient of inter-generational elasticity and Gini index on disposable income.
Source: Corak (2013), Krueger (2012)

3.4 Channels of inter-generational transmission of inequality

As we pointed out in chapter 1, the mainstream view of inequality has always argued that the diversity in income and wealth simply reflects the diversity of individuals' characteristics – knowledge, competences, productivity, entrepreneurial or financial skills, etc. – and is therefore fully justified. 'Human capital' is the concept that has been introduced in order to summarise such qualities, and it has also been used to account for the inter-generational transmission of disparities (Becker and Tomes, 1979, 1986; Solon, 2002).

This view rests on two hypotheses. The first one is that family background affects education (usually taken as a proxy for human capital) for several reasons: liquidity constraints in the presence of imperfect financial markets (Becker and Tomes, 1979, 1986), costless transmission of genetic traits and endowments (Becker and Tomes, 1979; Björklund *et al.*, 2005), peer effects (Benabou 1996) and educational policies (Schuetz *et al.*, 2008). A second hypothesis is that differences in earnings, as well as in occupational attainments, are the consequence of differences in human capital endowments. This assumption implies a labour market in which competition and merit prevail.

Given these two hypotheses, better family economic conditions imply a richer human capital endowment, which in turn brings higher earnings. So increasing inequality leads to a lower social mobility through a more unequal distribution of human capital.

Data do provide support for the first hypothesis. The evidence takes parental occupation as a proxy of family background. This choice is due to the paucity of reliable and comparable data on parental income. In any case, this choice is in line with a wealth of sociological literature that takes parental occupation as the best predictor of offspring outcomes.

The data suggest that everywhere there is a positive and highly significant association between parental background and educational attainment. More specifically, as shown in Figure 3.3, in all countries the probability of higher educational attainment is correlated with parental occupation. For example, in Italy the children of managers have a more than double probability than those of a production worker to get a university degree. In other countries the differential is less marked, but always very sizeable. The advantage accruing to the children of clerical workers is, as expected, smaller.

Since parents' income is correlated with their occupation, this evidence supports the hypothesis that family economic conditions exert a major influence on children's education. An obvious implication is that more unequal distribution of income will aggravate this effect, producing greater educational inequality.

The second hypothesis on which this explanation is based is more controversial. There is no doubt that human capital delivers a premium, in particular a university degree yields a substantial (but internationally differentiated) positive return. But this holds only on average. Actually, human capital is a risky investment and the variance in its returns is considerable. According to calculations (Franzini and Raitano, forthcoming), in all countries inequality within groups of people with the same educational level is much greater than inequality between groups with different educational levels.

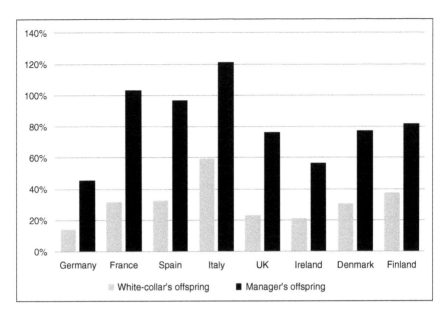

FIGURE 3.3 Inequality in education. Probability of attaining a university degree for children of white-collar and of managers with respect to children of blue-collar workers

Note: Probabilities computed as average partial effects from a logit model. Additional controls are gender, age, number of siblings and a dummy for the presence of both parents in the household when young. Offspring aged 35–49.
Source: Franzini and Raitano (forthcoming), data from EU-SILC 2005 survey

Such variance suggests that inequality in earnings is also the result of other factors that are not easy to identify. Indeed, from our point of view, the problem is to determine whether they are related to family background. An essential step is to check whether family background has an effect on offsprings' earnings over and above the one working via human capital. If it does, then there is good reason to believe not only that human capital cannot fully explain inequality, but also that at least some of the factors generating earnings inequality among equally educated people are, again, related to family background.

The ways in which families matter

The data on family background from the 2005 wave of the EU-SILC survey allow us to see whether parents' occupation has an additional influence, beyond that of educational attainment, on the earnings of their offspring. Figure 3.4, taken from Franzini and Raitano (2013), summarises the findings.

In almost all the countries, the additional influence of the family background is not negligible, and in some cases it is very sizeable indeed. In the UK, for example, the son of a manager earns 26 per cent more than the son of a blue-collar worker

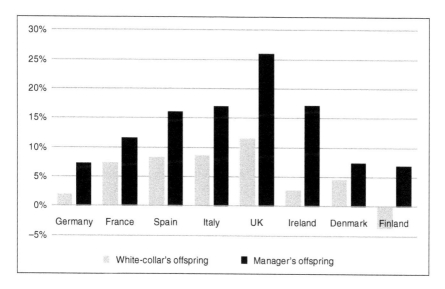

FIGURE 3.4 Inequality in earnings. Gross earnings gaps for children of white-collar and of managers with respect to children of blue-collar workers

Note: Estimated coefficients from an OLS model. Additional controls are gender, age, seniority and dummies for part-time, self-employment, immigrant and subjective health. Offspring aged 35–49. Results for Denmark, Finland, Germany and Ireland (white collars) and for Denmark and Finland (managers) are not significant at the 90% level.
Source: Franzini and Raitano (forthcoming), data from EU-SILC 2005 survey

even if they have the same level of education. In other countries, the gap is smaller, but significant: this is the case for Ireland, Italy, Spain and, to a lesser extent, France and Germany. The gap between white-collar and blue-collar offspring is smaller, but still significant, in the UK, Italy, Spain and France.

What could the other channels of influence be? Empirical evidence shows that among equally well-educated people the probability of having a managerial position depends on their parents' occupation. Everywhere, the probability is higher for the son of a manager than for the son of either a clerical or a production worker. In Finland, France, Denmark and the UK this gap is narrower. Also, the children of white collars have a general, though much smaller, advantage with respect to the children of blue-collar workers.

Moreover, if we control for both education and occupation, we again find that parents' occupation has an additional influence on the earnings of their offspring, at least in some countries. In other words, there is a residual effect of family background working directly on earnings, not indirectly through education and occupation.

In the UK this residual advantage enjoyed by the child of a manager over the child of a blue-collar worker amounts to about 15 per cent. Other countries where this advantage is statistically significant are Ireland, Italy and Spain. It is quite interesting that two Anglo-Saxon countries and two Mediterranean countries share this feature of the process that originates the inter-generational transmission of inequality.

Overall, family background can influence an individual's earnings in three ways: i) through the probability of attaining a higher level of education; ii) through the probability of achieving a good occupation; and iii) through a residual direct effect associated with both unobservable human capital and background-related market imperfections (Hudson and Sessions, 2011).

The first two channels are well known in the sociological literature on social mobility and are defined as 'achievement' and 'ascription' by Ganzeboom and Treiman (2007). The economic literature almost exclusively focuses on the first step. The third one is usually neglected despite its importance. Indeed, this direct, residual effect of family background, not mediated by education or occupation, appears as the main cause of cross-country differences in the magnitude of inter-generational inequality transmission.

This source of inequality has been investigated by Franzini *et al.* (2013), who found that in Nordic countries and Germany the influence of parental background on children's earnings is mostly mediated by indirect effects acting through formal education (achievement) and sorting into occupational macro-groups (ascription). The common belief is that these countries, characterised by generous welfare states, a regulated wage setting and well-functioning public education, offer more equal chances to all. In particular, Bratsberg *et al.* (2007) argue that good public education has created a high and homogenous human capital floor for all citizens, which has been essential to mitigate the direct family background effect on the working career.

In turn, in 'immobile' countries, large residual effects might reflect the impact of family background on the unobservable quality of education and family networks affecting workers' careers. The relative importance of these two mechanisms is likely to vary substantially across countries. In the UK, heterogeneous school quality and high skill premia should reinforce the first mechanism; in southern European countries, a non-transparent labour market selection (e.g. recommendations) should reinforce the second. However, data limitations do not allow an identification of these two mechanisms in a cross-country comparison. A more general conceptual framework is hence required for explaining cross-country differences in inter-generational inequality.

Soft skills and social contacts

The search for the factors that can explain the direct influence of family background on earnings can take three directions.

The first one involves the quality of human capital. The family background may play a part in determining several qualitative aspects of human capital that give a person an edge in the labour market. In the specific case of tertiary education, these may be the course of study chosen, the marks received or the particular university one attends.

The second one is soft skills, which include relational capacities such as attitudes to risk and trust, extroversion, the sense of discipline or leadership. These capacities, which are not strictly linked to human capital, would appear to be increasingly important at least in certain segments of the labour market (Bowles and Gintis, 2002; Goldthorpe and Jackson, 2008).

Both these directions point to what we can call unobservable characteristics or abilities. A good many scholars contend that wealthier and better-educated parents positively affect their children's unobservable abilities in several ways: selecting better schools, investing in extra-curricular activities, providing additional cultural inputs and transferring soft skills. Unfortunately it is virtually impossible to estimate directly the empirical relevance of these abilities.

The third and last direction turns towards networks of social contacts. There are many ways in which being a member of a privileged social group can secure an economic advantage.

One that is frequently stressed in the literature is quicker access to better information, especially on the availability of good jobs. Moreover, given their level of education, family networks can affect the probability of finding a good job or of being employed in different ways across countries (Pellizzari, 2010). For instance, well-off children can wait longer than less well-off children to find a good job, especially in systems with low unemployment benefits.

However, social networks can play a much more important role if the markets are, so to speak, not impartial; they can allow the sons of well-off families to get the best job and salary regardless of their abilities. As a result, in some cases workers with better abilities but lacking a supportive network of social contacts can be left out. Social contacts can therefore have a profound allocative effect, with negative consequences not only on economic mobility but also on efficiency. Family background is a key factor in this case. One's network of social contacts is essentially those of the family of origin; and the quality of such networks is positively correlated with the social status and the economic conditions of the family itself. In sum, there are sound arguments for the case that unobservable abilities and social contacts could both account for the residual background effect not explained by occupation and education.

We may be able to gain insight into the likely importance of the two factors in different countries by comparing what happens to the people who improve their social position from one generation to the next and to those whose position deteriorates. More precisely, those who improve their position may well experience an earning gap from the average wage of individuals with the same characteristics; those who slip down the scale of occupations may still maintain above average earnings. If there are penalties for upward mobility (after controlling for human capital) we can talk of a glass ceiling effect, while a parachute effect may be at work if downward mobility is buffered by a sort of invisible insurance.

Estimates of the glass ceiling and parachute effects in eight European countries (Raitano and Vona, 2011) show that in the UK and Ireland there is a significant glass ceiling effect, but no parachute effect. Southern European countries differ sharply;

especially in Italy, where there is a strong parachute effect insuring the children of the better-off against too sharp a loss when they go down the occupation ladder. In particular, the blue-collar worker who is the son of a manager earns significantly more than one whose father is also a blue-collar worker. In Germany and France insignificant residual background associations coexist with penalties for both downward and upward mobility. In Nordic countries no clear pattern emerges.

These findings, along with the assumption that parachute effects are the consequence of effective networks of social contacts, suggest that in Italy and Spain social networks are likely to be essential in explaining the residual background effect, while in Britain unobservable abilities appear to be more important.

3.5 Equality of opportunity across generations

The inter-generational transmission of inequality prevents social and economic mobility and is considered a negative feature of our society. But we can ask: would a society with zero transmission be a really desirable one?

In order to answer this question we have to link the inter-generational transmission of inequality to the equality of opportunity, which is widely seen as an acceptable form of equality. Having a zero transmission of income inequality is fully acceptable if all the advantages coming from family background are unjustified. Looking into the equality of opportunity literature, we can classify such advantages and evaluate them in terms of their acceptability. As Swift (2005: 7) argues, from the perspective of equality of opportunity inequalities that are as a result of factors beyond individual control are not acceptable – following Roemer (1998) we could call them circumstances. Conversely, effort is a just cause of inequality. Following Roemer (2004) we can list the most important factors of inequality. There are, first of all, genetic abilities and traits such as intelligence, health, physical look; then we have competences and knowledge acquired during formal education or through the influence of the family background. Further factors of inequality are individual aspirations and cultural values, as well as personal preferences that also influence the effort put into the work. Finally, there are the social networks to which one has access that may strongly influence the chances of getting higher earnings, as we have already recalled.

To classify each of these factors as a circumstance (generating unacceptable inequality) or effort (viewed as a cause of just inequality) is not a simple task; in fact, opinions may vary widely. An extreme position is to argue that all these factors are to be considered as circumstances and, therefore, no inequality in the outcomes is acceptable. As Roemer (2009: 31) puts it, in this case nobody would be responsible for anything and we should stand for the equality of outcomes.

The opposite extreme position is when it is assumed that individual responsibility lies behind all these factors, so that inequality is always fully acceptable. Both these views are clearly untenable. Could we accept laziness on the argument that it is the result of preferences for which the holder bears no responsibility? Or should we really aim at nullifying the influence of any genetically transmitted trait? As

Swift (2005) argues, some of such traits are constitutive of human identity. Moreover, cultural values can be intentionally transmitted by the family and the claim that they should have no effect on the life prospect of the children is equivalent to arguing that the role of the family itself has to be reshaped.

Between these extreme positions a compromise should be found. A reasonable view could be to consider as unacceptable both the advantages coming from families' social networks and the disadvantages coming from the inability to improve one's own human capital because of a poor family background. Inequalities stemming from these two factors appear as a violation of a fair idea of equality of opportunity.

We can now link this analysis to the transmission of economic inequality. The first step is to recognise that all the listed factors of inequality, with the only exception of individual effort, are related to family income. Advocating zero transmission of inequality amounts, therefore, to treating all those factors as unacceptable, which is not easy to argue, as we have seen. So we can conclude that no inter-generational transmission (i.e. perfect social mobility) is not the same thing as equality of opportunity (if the latter is properly defined). The compatibility between these two conceptions would be possible if the two unacceptable factors identified above (i.e. the advantage from social networks and the disadvantage from economic barriers to education) are eliminated, and richer families are not allowed to transfer to their sons and daughters an advantage under these two channels.

The problem of how to avoid these unacceptable inequalities is not an easy one. The strategy could be either to prevent them from arising (and this seems to be easier in the case of barriers to education) or to compensate for them once they have materialised.

But there is a further problem to consider: the way markets actually work. Frequently markets do not treat people exerting the same effort and with the same competences in the same way. If this is the case, equalising opportunities will not guarantee that only acceptable inequalities will ensue. In this case, markets are not impartial, as implicitly assumed by most scholars of equality of opportunity. Partial markets can allow social contacts to play a role, which would be neither fair nor efficient. Favourable social networks could yield higher compensations independently from any merit-based advantage; if family income is conducive to such favourable contacts, the result is precisely the inter-generational transmission of unacceptable inequalities. Therefore, any policy intervention that can make markets more impartial is also a policy that can reduce the transmission of unacceptable inequalities. Of course, the vulnerability of markets to social contacts is not of the same degree in all countries, as the data we have seen seem to suggest.

Limiting the transmission of unacceptable inequalities demands also other measures, including making it easier for people coming from a poor background to get higher education and better competences.

In conclusion, inequality is transmitted from one generation to the next through the inheritance of wealth and, more subtly, through the various advantages that a better family background can offer in the labour market. Both are key elements of the model of 'oligarch capitalism' that we have identified as one of the engines of today's inequality. The conceptual arguments and the evidence provided in this chapter offer a better understanding of the mechanisms at work and of the policy actions that could be taken to reverse the unacceptable – and dangerous – inequality transmitted across generations by wealth and privilege.

Notes

1   β, is estimated by regressing offsprings' log income on parents'. On the β coefficient see, among others, Björklund and Jäntti (2009) and Blanden (2013).
2   Among others, let us mention Solon (2002) and Corak (2006). The data presented are taken from Corak (2013).

4

EXPLAINING INEQUALITY

4.1 Introduction

Inequality is an apparently easy, but in fact slippery, concept. We have seen that we need to define it carefully, measure it with appropriate data and relate it to relevant phenomena. In chapter 2 we have documented the distance between classes and social groups – in the distribution of income between capital and labour and in the rise of top incomes – disparities between individuals and households in various income measures, differences between high- and low-skilled workers, disparities at the global level in the income of the world's citizens and inequality in wealth. Distances can be measured in several dimensions and inequality can emerge not just in income or wealth, but also in terms of rights, capabilities, access to services and measures of wellbeing. In chapter 3 the role of families and the inter-generational dimension of inequality have been highlighted, with the importance of heritage in shaping wealth and family background in shaping incomes.

The evidence on the general rise of inequality in these different dimensions, however, calls for a deeper interpretation of its causes; the economic, social and political processes that produced such growing disparities need be identified, providing an explanation of the 'engines of inequality' that are at work in advanced countries.

This chapter explores how the power of capital over labour, the rise of oligarch capitalism and the individualisation of economic conditions – three of the engines of inequality presented in chapter 1 – can explain the rise of disparities. The final chapter of this book will address the fourth mechanism – the retreat of politics – and will provide a range of policy proposals to reverse the rise of inequality.

4.2 The dynamics of capital

The functional distribution of income between wages and profits is a fundamental process shaping inequalities among social classes and groups receiving different types of income. We have seen in chapter 2 that, since 1980, most advanced countries have experienced a significant reduction of the labour share in GDP, of the order of 10 percentage points. What are the forces leading to such a substantial distributional shift?

At first sight, since the 1980s a wide range of developments have gone in the direction of expanding the power of capital – the first engine of inequality. First, the liberalisation of capital movements has led to a surge of capital flows – for foreign direct investment and for the acquisition of financial assets – driven by a search for higher profits. Second, the growth of financial activities – the most profitable, mobile and volatile form of capital – has dominated investment patterns. In the US the ratio of aggregate profits of the financial sector to profits of non-financial activities has increased from 20 per cent in the 1970s to 50 per cent after 2000 (Glyn, 2006: ch. 3). The expansion of finance has led to the creation of increasingly complex markets for credit, stocks, bonds, real estate, currencies, futures, commodities, derivatives, etc., driven by a search for short-term speculative gains and leading to major bubbles – and to the financial collapse of 2008. Third, international production systems have emerged as a result of the use of new technologies – in information and communication and other fields – and of the freedom of movement of capital; this has greatly reduced the power – and the employment – of labour in advanced countries, with a corresponding fall in wages. We need to understand in which specific ways these developments affect inequality.

Piketty's capital and beyond

Useful starting points in this investigation are the mechanisms identified by Piketty (2013) as 'fundamental laws of capitalism'. In his view the rise of the capital share (α = profits/income) is the necessary result of the high rate of return to capital (r) and of the rise of the capital/income ratio (β) ($\alpha = r \cdot \beta$, his 'first law of capitalism'). In turn, the growing capital/income ratio goes hand in hand with a stable propensity to save (s) and the slowdown in income growth (g) as a result of stagnation in population and slow rise of productivity ($\beta = s/g$, his 'second law of capitalism'). Let us address these relationships one by one.

Returns to capital greater than the rate of growth (r > g)

In the conceptual framework of Piketty, a key driver of the rise in inequality is the fact that in recent decades the rate of return to capital (r = profits/capital)[1] has been higher than the rate of growth of the economy (g). His current estimate is that the rate of return on total capital is close to 5 per cent, while GDP growth rates in advanced countries have rarely gone beyond 2 per cent. Taking a longer view, and considering Britain, Piketty estimates that the average rate of return to capital (net of the effort needed to manage investment) has oscillated between 4 and 5 per cent from 1770 to 1930, moving up close to 7 per cent in 1940 and then falling to just above 3 per cent in 1980 and 1990, before a new rise above 4 per cent. In France he finds oscillations between 4 and 6 per cent, with 7 per cent peaks in 1920 and 1950 (Piketty, 2013: 318, Graphs 6.3 and 6.4).[2] The gap with GDP growth is significant; a 5 per cent growth rate of advanced economies has been achieved only in exceptional cases.

This r > g gap has two implications. First, if at least some of the returns to capital are invested to expand it, the accumulation of capital proceeds at a faster pace than economic growth, resulting in growing capital/income ratios. Second, the amount of profits paid to capital has to increase; when GDP increases at a slower pace than the rate of profit, a growing share of income has to go to capital, reducing the wage share. Higher inequalities are therefore the result of the importance of capital and the slowdown of growth.

The rise in the capital/income ratio

The value of capital expressed in years of national income is now between 5 and 6 times in the UK and France, 4.5 times in the US and 4 times in Germany. France and the UK are ap proaching the levels typical of the early twentieth century – in 1870–1910 the level was close to 7; the two world wars brought it down to less than 3 in 1950, with a continuous rise since then. In the US the trend has been more stable, with peaks of 5 in 1910 and 1930, a fall to less than 4 in 1950 and a constant rise since then (Piketty, 2013: 234–9). Piketty emphasises the drive towards a greater role of capital and concludes that 'there is no natural force that will necessarily reduce the importance of capital and of the incomes resulting from the ownership of capital in the course of history' (2013: 370). In other words – short of major shocks or world wars – the growth in the share of income going to capital, and the resulting inequality, is unlikely to be reversed.

There are, however, three critical issues in the analysis of Piketty. First, the heterogeneity of capital and the diversity between productive capital and financial wealth; second, the specific nature of financial accumulation and the cyclical nature of capitalist growth; and third, the ways we understand the process of economic growth. We consider them in turn.

Productive capital vs. financial and real estate wealth

A controversial question in the analysis of Piketty is his definition of capital:

> capital is defined as the sum total of nonhuman assets that can be owned and exchanged on some market. Capital includes all forms of real property (including residential real estate) as well as financial and professional capital

(plants, infrastructure, machinery, patents and so on) used by firms and government agencies.

(Piketty, 2013: 82)

This definition does not distinguish between productive capital and non-productive wealth. In fact he also writes: 'I use the word capital and wealth interchangeably as if they were perfectly synonymous' (2013: 84). He is aware that the composition of capital has changed over time, from the dominance of agricultural land in the past, to real estate, business and financial assets today. And he documents that different types of capital have different returns – the average long-run rate of return on stocks is 7 to 8 per cent in many countries, investment in real estate and bonds yields a 3–4 per cent return, while the real rate of interest on public debt is usually much lower (2013: 94) – but he focuses on the resulting aggregate rate of return on capital, that is about 5 per cent.

From the point of view of income distribution this choice can be appropriate in order to identify the returns going to all forms of capital. But when we look at production, increased output is in fact the result of increased productive capital alone. An increase in the value of financial assets – and of a given real estate – does not help expand output. It does change the distribution of income as a result of high returns on capital – that can be transferred from industrial profits to financial and real estate rents – or of speculative bubbles that inflate asset prices. Therefore, if the expansion of capital is a result of growing values of non-productive assets, it becomes difficult to expect rising output with a rising productivity of capital, and rising rates of profits.[3]

A deeper understanding of the relationships between productive and financial capital in the process of accumulation is needed, therefore, before addressing the roots of the current slowdown in growth.[4]

The dynamics of finance

In order to put in perspective the findings of Piketty, we can refer to the analysis of accumulation as a succession of cycles proposed by Giovanni Arrighi (1994) – drawing from Marx, and Braudel (1979). In this view, the first part of the cycle of accumulation is characterised by a material expansion, rooted in technological advances and high demand for new products and industries, with growing trade and production as money is turned into productive capital, embodied in a particular set of means of production. The material expansion at first produces large monopolistic profits. Then more capital is invested in the same activities without a parallel increase in the opportunities for profits, resulting in greater competition and a lowering profit rate. This leads to a 'signal' crisis – a recession associated to inadequate profits – that may destroy the least productive capital. After that, capitalists decide to hold a larger share of capital in the form of liquid assets, creating the conditions for a period of financial expansion – the second part of the cycle – in which capital searches for profits without going through material investment. The supply of money capital soars, alongside the demand for liquidity and debt, due also to the impact of the crisis on public and private finances. The financial expansion produces a period of renewed growth, but capital accumulation cannot be sustained indefinitely by financial investment and speculative bubbles in stock markets and real estate prices. When bubbles burst, the accumulated debt of firms and governments become unsustainable, banks fail and the economic crash may turn into a protracted depression – the 'terminal crisis' of the accumulation cycle. After the depression, new economic and political conditions can lead to the emergence of a new cycle of growth.

For Arrighi, capitalism has developed since its start through a sequence of cycles of accumulation that are paralleled by a succession of hegemonic cycles in the sphere of political relations among states; each hegemony represents the centre of the specific world system in which capitalism is organised (Braudel, 1979; Wallerstein, 1974). This interpretation suggests that, in the current period of US hegemony, the phase of material expansion started with the Second World War and reached its 'signal crisis' in the 1970s, followed by the phase of financial expansion started in 1980 that has led to the crisis of 2008 and the current stagnation. Building on this perspective, back in 1999 – at the height of the American expansion powered by the 'new economy' and finance – Arrighi and Silver could argue that:

> The global financial expansion of the last twenty years or so … is the clearest sign that we are in the midst of a hegemonic crisis. As such, the expansion can be expected to be a temporary phenomenon that will end more or less catastrophically, depending on how the crisis is handled by the declining hegemon.
> *(Arrighi and Silver, 1999: 272; see also Pianta, 2012: 12)*

These insights on the cycles of accumulation can integrate the analysis of Piketty on the growth of capital/income ratio; the peaks of such ratio – 1910–1930 and 2010 – are indeed the peaks of the phases of financial expansion where the value of capital is inflated by bubbles. Conversely, the decades from 1950 to 1980 – with the lowest capital/income ratios – are the period of the fastest growth of material production and income.

Piketty himself shows the importance of finance in today's capital when he demonstrates that total financial assets and liabilities have grown much faster than net wealth. In most countries the sum of financial assets and liabilities was equal to four or five years of national income in the 1970s; in 2010 it is between 10 and 15 years in the US, France, Germany and Japan, reaching 20 years in the UK (Piketty, 2013: 305). This expansion of financial assets and debts comes from the escalating complexity of financial operations, cross-ownership deals, bank lending, etc.

A more specific measure of the growing role of finance is the rise in the ratio between market and book value of corporations. At the end of the 1970s it ranged everywhere from 30 to 50 per cent; in 2010 it was close to 120 per cent in the

UK, 100 per cent in the US and 80 per cent in France – only Germany and Japan, with different ownership and financial systems, stayed at around 50 per cent. At the peak of the 1999 financial bubble an extreme value of 150 per cent was recorded for the UK (Piketty, 2013: 297). This rise of finance has clearly marked the current expansion of capital values, driven also by the emphasis on 'shareholder value' in the management of firms, an approach that has led corporations to give priority to rising stock prices – using stock buybacks as a key tool – distributing dividends to shareholders and super-bonuses to top managers while at the same time cutting back on material and R&D investment that provide the basis for sustained growth (Lazonick, 2015). Other insights on the dynamics of finance (Chesnais, 2004; Lapavitsas, 2013) could enrich the analysis of the current phase of finance-driven accumulation.

The very nature of such financial expansion is unlikely to be sustainable. Rather than an indefinite rise of the importance of capital – with expanding finance and growing capital/income ratios and capital shares in national income – we could expect developments and crises that will affect – and eventually limit – the role of finance. Piketty is right, however, to emphasise that the distribution of income between profits and wages is, in the end, the outcome of the balance of power between capital and labour 'The price of capital … is always in part a social and political construction: it reflects the idea of ownership prevailing in society and depends on multiple policies and institutions regulating relationships between the different social groups concerned' (Piketty, 2013: 296).

In fact, the years of low capital/income ratios and fast growth – from 1950 to 1980 – were characterised, especially in Europe, by clear political constraints on the accumulation of capital and on returns from investment, including strict control over international capital movements, tight regulation on finance, extensive public ownership of large firms in key industries, rent control policies, planning controls on real estate and high taxation on profits, rents and top incomes. These policies limited the returns to capital and the share of profits in national income. Most of them were cancelled or drastically reduced in the neoliberal era starting in the 1980s. Since then the greater power of capital has made sure that it obtains high returns from the variety of possible investments – from global production to speculative finance – even when actual production capacities are not developed. The power of capital will have to be confronted, and many of the policies limiting returns to capital will have to be reintroduced – as we will see in the final chapter – if we want to reverse the current rise in inequality.

The dynamics of growth

We have already seen that, in Piketty's explanation of inequality, a key role is played by the fact that the rate of return to capital (r) is higher than the rate of growth of the economy (g). But what are the sources of the economy's growth? This is a crucial – and highly debated – issue in economics; Piketty builds here on mainstream growth theories[5] and investigates the growth trajectories of advanced countries.

In empirical terms, the growth rate of national income can be decomposed as the sum of the increase in population and in per capita income (as aggregate income equals aggregate product, the latter can be interpreted as a measure of average productivity). In all advanced countries in the 1970–2010 period growth rates have declined compared with 1950–1970. On average, they fell to 2.8 per cent per year in the US (resulting from a 1 per cent population increase and a 1.8 per capita income growth), 2.5 per cent in Japan, 2.2 per cent in France and the UK, 2 per cent in Germany and 1.9 per cent in Italy. In Europe and Japan these performances resulted from a lower population growth of 0.3 to 0.5 per cent, and from per capita income growth ranging from 2 per cent in Japan to 1.6 per cent in Italy (Piketty, 2013: 275, Table 5.1). The slowdown in the growth of product per capita has been significant – in the period 1950–1970 its average annual growth was above 4 per cent in Europe and 2.3 per cent in the US (Piketty, 2013: 163, Graph 2.3).

At the same time, Piketty's estimates for the adjusted rates of return to capital for the UK and France range from 6–7 per cent in 1950 to 4 per cent in 2010 – much higher values that the rates of growth of national income (2013: 318, Graphs 6.3 and 6.4). According to this evidence, a larger amount of capital has been able to command a high rate of return – greater than the rate of growth of the economy – even if with some decline in more recent years, also as a result of the crisis. The result of such dynamics has been the systematic growth in the share of capital in national income that we have seen in Figure 2.2 in chapter 2.[6]

In his outlook for the future, at the world level Piketty expects that the growth of world output will be on average about 1.5 per cent per year, while the saving rate will be about 10 per cent. As savings and investment have to be equal, and assuming that the pace of growth of capital and income will be the same, this implies – on the basis of $\beta = s/g$ – that the capital/output ratio will go up to almost seven (10/1.5), a record level for the world as a whole. In other words, the prospect for Piketty is a generalisation of the importance of capital, with growing capital/output ratios, shares of profit in income and inequality in the world economy. This increase in the concentration of capital will converge to a level that will be higher the larger is the gap between r and g (2013: 308–9, Graph 5.8).

There are, however, a few objections that can be raised to such a view. First, as seen above – following Marx, Schumpeter and Arrighi – the accumulation of capital proceeds in cycles and the current financial expansion is unlikely to continue indefinitely and extend at the world level. In fact accumulation has always relied on strong asymmetries between centre and periphery at the world level. Therefore, the general rise in the value of capital may soon return to its cyclical pattern.

Second – following Keynes – demand matters. Accumulation of capital and income growth requires a demand that is able to absorb production. At the world level demand is the result of the distribution of income between profits – generally leading to savings and investment – and wages, turned into consumption. If total wages fall, not even the opulent consumption of the richest 10 per cent with rising incomes will be adequate to assure the necessary demand. With lower total consumption, the savings of the world's richest will increase, but where will they be invested? It is unlikely that they will be turned into productive investment when demand is stagnant. Financial assets may indeed multiply indefinitely, but then it would be increasingly difficult to make sure that their returns are high when the world productive base stagnates (this points out again the problem in Piketty's identification between capital and wealth).

Third, – following growth theories – we need to understand how the production process that generates income, profit and wages is conceptualised. Piketty relies on the neoclassical growth model where capital and labour are combined – originally on the basis of fixed coefficients – in order to obtain output, while the technology is exogenous. Robert Solow – a key founder of this approach – argued that:

> As production becomes more and more capital-intensive, it gets harder and harder to find profitable uses for additional capital, or easy ways to substitute capital for labour. Whether the capital share falls or rises depends on whether the rate of return has to fall proportionally more or less than the capital/income rises.
>
> *(Solow, 2014)*

If capital becomes more abundant, in other words, are we sure that capital can continue to replace labour – and therefore reduce employment and wages – while assuring the same output growth? In fact, neoclassical views of production factors have traditionally argued that the returns to capital or labour fall when the production factor is more abundant. In this case, an increase in the capital/income ratio would lead to a fall in the rate of profit and a slowdown in capital accumulation. Piketty's way out of this problem is the assumption that the same output increase can be achieved with an increase in the amount of capital that is higher than the increase of the amount of labour – that is, the elasticity of substitution between capital and labour is greater than one (Piketty, 2015: 81).

This type of neoclassical model assumes that the returns obtained by capital and labour reflect their marginal productivities; a greater amount of more productive capital can thus gain higher returns and a larger share of total income. There are several questions that could be raised here. First, there are serious uncertainties on the possibility to measure capital and on the identification between capital and wealth made by Piketty (as discussed above). Second, most of the recorded growth in advanced countries is not a result of increases in the quantity of capital and labour, but of change in technology that is not exogenous, but is developed by deliberate choices, requiring specific qualities of capital and labour in combinations that cannot be varied at will (you cannot have an automated factory run by workers with no ICT skills). Third, when production is characterised by economies of scale – increases in output are greater that increases in inputs – the rate of profit (r) and the growth rate of incomes (g) can move hand in hand, but the capital/output ratio is likely to fall, not rise.

In a follow-up article some of these points are addressed (Piketty, 2015). First, greater attention is devoted to the conditions that are required for the relations discussed above to emerge. A rate of return of capital (r) greater than the rate of growth of the economy (g) leads to higher disparities in particular when, as pointed out by Solow (2014), 'the income and wealth of the rich will grow faster than the typical income from work'. This is a reasonable assumption as the return on capital tends to be larger for owners of larger amounts of capital, introducing an additional mechanism of concentration of income and wealth.[7]

Second, Piketty acknowledges that not all capital and production processes are the same. He acknowledges that 'large upward or downward movements of real estate prices play an important role in the evolution of aggregate capital values during recent decades' and suggests that 'the right model to think about rising capital–income ratios and capital shares in recent decades is a multi-sector model of capital accumulation, with substantial movements in relative prices, and with important variations in bargaining power over time' (2015: 52). Such research direction may highlight the different dynamics of production and distribution within the economy, addressing also the specificity of productive and non-productive capital.

Third, more attention is devoted to the role of labour income. He argues that r > g cannot be considered as 'a useful tool for the discussion of rising inequality of labor income: other mechanisms and policies are much more relevant here, e.g. supply and demand of skills and education' (2015: 48).

Without entering into a detailed discussion, we can conclude that the key relationships identified by Piketty between the capital/income ratio, the rate of profit, the rate of growth and resulting inequality are important points of reference identifying the dynamics of capitalism, but have to be qualified with more specific theories, more realistic assumptions and empirical investigations focusing on specific historical contexts. In the next section we propose a conceptual framework that can accommodate the dynamics of capital and the growth of income discussed above with the four engines of inequality we have identified.

4.3 Capital, income and the engines of inequality

The arguments of the previous section can be summarised in Figure 4.1, where the parallel dynamics of capital and income are presented. The aim is to identify the key mechanisms and the causal links that explain the 'stylised facts' on capital, growth and inequality. Building on our discussion of Piketty's work in the previous section, we propose to introduce the distinction between productive capital – the assets that are used for producing goods and services, including buildings, machinery and intangible capital – and financial wealth – assets granting a monetary return, whose nature of rent-seeking investment prevails over the contribution they offer to the production of new output. We are well aware that this is a problematic distinction, at the centre of extensive debates in economic literature; what we want to introduce here is simply a conceptual distinction in the aggregate definition of capital as wealth by Piketty (2013) between two components with different dynamics of accumulation. First, capital used for production activities

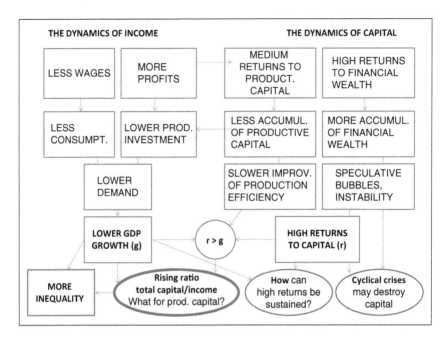

FIGURE 4.1 The dynamics of income and the dynamics of productive and financial capital

directly contributes to GDP growth and generates profits when production is successful; its accumulation comes from the flow of reinvested profits and its real effects may include an expansion of capacity and an improvement of productivity and efficiency. Second, financial assets generate rents that are drawn from national income and subtracted from the earnings of labour and productive capital. The accumulation of financial wealth mainly proceeds from the inflation of asset values and speculative bubbles; this may have an indirect impact on GDP dynamics through wealth effects, but it introduces a greater instability and a risk of financial crisis. We do not attempt here an empirical definition of productive capital and financial wealth. Several components – for instance corporate stock and bonds – combine both characteristics. A particularly complex issue is that of real estate assets; homes can be used by owners, generating imputed income, can be rented, generating economic activities, can be bought and sold in order to obtain capital gains and can be used as collateral for financial transactions. Similar complexities appear in the case of offices and plants that can be used for carrying out production, but also for finance-oriented operations.

The conceptual distinction between productive capital and financial wealth makes it possible to understand the divergent dynamics pointed out in the previous section between the moderate returns to productive capital and the very high returns to financial wealth. In aggregate, they result in historically high returns to capital (r) that are greater than the rate of growth of GDP (g).

The latter, however, is directly affected by the slower accumulation of productive capital that results in lower investment, demand and growth; moreover, this lack of productive capital slows down the improvements in productivity that are needed to sustain growth.

What are the implications of this framework on the mechanisms identified by Piketty? First, the rise in the capital/income ratio may be heavily affected by the expansion of financial wealth alone; the productive capital/income ratio is significantly lower and could be more stable. Second, how can such high returns to capital be sustained? Profits on productive capital may slow down with slower accumulation and growth. High rents on financial wealth are sustained by inflating asset values, and may impose an excessive burden on profits and wages as GDP growth slows down; all this may increase instability. Third, the inflating value of financial (and real estate) assets may at some point lead to a burst of the speculative bubble – as happened in 2008. This may open up a downswing of the economic cycle where some of the previously inflated asset values are lost, reducing the capital/income ratio – as in the Great Depression of the 1930s.

We can now address the dynamics of income and growth considering the left side of Figure 4.1. In chapter 2 we have documented the rise in the capital share; this is the base for the high returns to productive capital and financial wealth. A falling wage share and a higher income inequality, however, result in lower consumption and lower multiplying effects of demand, contributing to a slowdown of growth. The same effect emerges when investment is mainly directed towards financial rather than productive activities. A lower growth rate is indeed facing higher returns to capital (r > g). As profits and rents have to be paid out of national income – as we already pointed out – in the longer term a lower growth could make the same high returns unsustainable. The only possibility with a stagnant GDP is an ever increasing capital share and a parallel fall of wages, resulting in ever increasing inequality – until some drastic social and political development may put an end to such capitalist dynamics.

Summing up, this framework allows us to identify the implications for inequality of the broader dynamics of capital and income. Inequality increases when profits rise more than wages; when returns to capital – inflated by financial assets – are higher than growth rates; and when a financial expansion leads to high rents that put pressure on the functional distribution of income, reducing the wage share. All these developments – from the expansion of finance to growing inequality – can hardly be expected to follow a linear trajectory; historical experience has shown that capital accumulation follows a cyclical pattern, that its contradictions lead to cyclical crises and that changes in social and political relations can affect the future of inequality – and capitalism.

The impact of the engines of inequality

Building on this framework, we can move to investigate the specific mechanisms generating inequality, identified in Figure 4.2. Again, here we are mainly concerned with a conceptual definition that has to come before empirical investigations of the

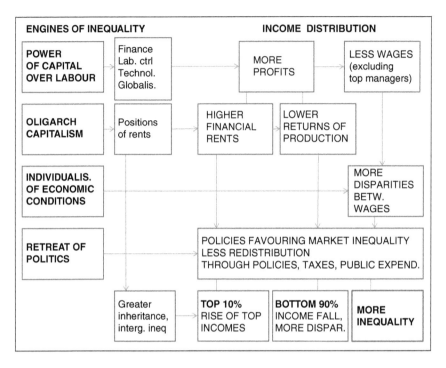

FIGURE 4.2 The four engines of inequality and their impact on income distribution

particular impact of each engine of inequality. As we already made clear in chapter 1, the four engines of inequality operate at different levels and closely interact with one another. However, Figure 4.2 provides a simplified summary of their inegalitarian effects on different economic and policy processes.

The first engine of inequality – the power of capital over labour – has a direct impact on the functional distribution of income, leading to higher profits and lower wages (for the sake of logical coherence, here we exclude from wages the remuneration of top managers). There are, however, several specific processes through which this impact takes place. The rise of finance is a major one, as we have seen in the previous section. The ability of capital to control labour and decide its use – changing quantity and quality of employment, controlling work practices, increasing intensity of efforts, setting lower wages, etc. – is a second key factor weakening labour and leading to a lower wage share in national income. The use of technological change, and ICTs in particular, for creating new products and markets with high Schumpeterian profits, for increasing control over production and labour and for labour-saving (and wage-saving) new processes is a third mechanism associated to the power of capital. Finally, capital's ability to organise production at a global scale has increased profit opportunities and has put workers of advanced and emerging countries in competition with one another, resulting in a lowering of wages in richer economies. In section 4.4 these mechanisms are examined on the basis of the available evidence.

The second engine of inequality is the emergence of an oligarch capitalism characterised by the concentration of income, wealth and power in the top 10 per cent of citizens – and most notably in the ultra rich top 1 per cent. This is the result of the control that such a group – largely made of top managers – has on income flows, returns to capital and positions of rent that have nothing to do with economic merit or productivity. They are able to capture a larger share of income in the forms of rents, financial returns and top labour compensation, reducing resources for wages and for profits reinvested in production capacity. At the top of the distribution, wealth is even more concentrated than income and is largely transmitted through inheritance, reproducing an oligarchy of money that makes today's capitalism increasingly similar to the *ancien régime*. The impact on inequality is visible in the rise of the top 10 per cent of incomes, in the growing concentration of wealth and in the greater importance of inheritance in shaping the distribution of wealth, as we will see in section 4.5.

The third engine of growth is the individualisation of economic and social conditions, with a breakdown of collective identities, leading to greater disparities within wages – even after we exclude the compensation of top managers. A lower wage share is distributed among workers that are increasingly divided in terms of family backgrounds, education and employment contracts – permanent or temporary, full-time or part-time, etc. – and are polarised in terms of skills and wages. As we will see in section 4.6, these mechanisms introduce greater inequality among wage earners and among the bottom 90 per cent of incomes.

Finally, the fourth mechanism of inequality is the retreat of politics. This is the result of changed political power relations and of policy views that have reduced the role of the State and expanded the range of market processes, resulting in higher inequalities. Moreover, the retreat of politics has reduced the space for redistribution through taxes, public expenditure and provision of public services outside the market. The other three engines of inequality have also had an impact on the reduced room for redistribution. As shown in Figure 4.2, the power of capital and the emergence of oligarch capitalism are associated to the rise of profits and, in particular, of highly mobile financial rents. This reduces the tax base a country can rely on, as fiscal havens are increasingly used for tax evasion and elusion by corporations and the rich. The weakening and individualisation of labour reduces the wage share of national income that is already significantly taxed with very low progressivity; resources for redistribution can hardly come from such a source. Moreover, the greater fragmentation of labour makes it difficult to have a consensus on the possibility of carrying out a significant redistribution within wage earners. The reduction or cancellation of inheritance taxes favours the inter-generational transmission of huge wealth disparities. Again, the overall outcome of the retreat of politics and of reduced redistribution is the rise of the top 10 per cent and the fall of a more fragmented bottom 90 per cent. Section 4.7 and chapter 5 will address these challenges.

4.4 The power of capital over labour

In the last three decades economic, social and political processes have shaped this change in the balance of power between capital and labour with far reaching consequences on the rise of inequality. However, we need to identify the specific mechanisms that, in a context more favourable to capital, have reorganised the economic system and its inegalitarian outcomes. In Figure 4.2 we consider the four most important ones – finance, the control over labour, technological change and globalisation.

The power of finance

The rise of finance – and the greater importance of financial wealth as opposed to productive capital – is the specific form taken by the power of capital in the last three decades. Section 4.2 has already discussed at length the dynamics of capital and the characteristics – and dangers – of financial accumulation. The implications for inequality have already been documented, moving on from the work of Piketty (2013); they include the higher concentration of income and wealth at the top of the distribution and the lower wage share in national income.

The control over labour

The relationship between capital and labour is the fundamental relation of capitalism, at the source of the accumulation of capital and of the class division of society. The evolution of capitalism has been largely shaped by the conflict between the logic of capital accumulation and workers' efforts in asserting labour and social rights. In particular, workers demand the right to organise in unions, higher wages from collective labour contracts, employment security, reduced working hours, safer working conditions, greater control over the pace and content of work, social insurance, welfare protection and sometimes even workplace democracy and some control over business decision making.

These multiple dimensions show how the whole society is affected by capital–labour relations. In fact, the capital–labour conflict is not played out in workplaces alone; public policies reflect this balance of forces and introduce legislation that may expand or reduce the protection of labour and social rights. Labour legislation can provide guidelines on employment contracts, wage setting and minimum wages that have direct effects on the distribution of income and inequality. As we have already pointed out, in advanced countries the post-war decades have been a period of expanding labour rights; conversely, since 1980 a broad reversal in legislation and capital–labour relations has led to worsening conditions for workers. Glyn (2006: ch. 5) provides an effective overview of 'labour's retreat' in the last decades in terms of job losses, work hours and intensity and wages and union power.[8] We address here some issues where the ascendancy of capital has led to greater control over labour. In section 4.6 attention will be devoted to the individualisation of labour as an additional engine of inequality.

The starting point here is the functional distribution of income between wages and profits – the most immediate indicator of the balance of forces between labour and capital. In chapter 2 we have documented that in advanced countries in the last decades more than 10 percentage points of national income have shifted from wages to profits, resulting in a major increase in inequality. Real wages have fallen for most workers, in most countries and industries. Labour has been less able to capture an adequate share of the economy's productivity gains. Since 2003 one-third of European workers have experienced a decline in real wages, and almost two-thirds saw their wages growing, on average, less than their labour productivity (Bogliacino, 2009).

These outcomes, however, result from a combination of factors that may weaken workers, employment and wages. The 2012 OECD Employment Outlook argued that the reduction in the labour share was linked to labour-displacing technological change, to a rise in domestic and foreign competition – including delocalisation and imports that replace national production – and to the reduction of public ownership through privatisations. The report suggested that 'the reduction in the labour share associated with domestic and foreign competition and reduction of public ownership could be partly explained by their effect on workers bargaining power' (OECD, 2012: 111). Moreover, it argued that greater competitive pressure reduced the coverage of collective bargaining systems and the role and membership of trade unions; more workers have their wages set outside national collective contracts negotiated by the unions and local or individual bargaining increases wage dispersion. All this 'probably explains part of the deterioration of low-skilled workers' position' (OECD, 2012).

The evolution of workers' bargaining power is closely associated to the importance of trade unions in organising labour, negotiating labour contracts and obtaining better conditions. It has been shown that a stronger union presence is conducive to lower inequalities within wages and in the economy as a whole (Card et al., 2003; Visser and Checchi, 2009; Checchi et al., 2010). Associated aspects include the extent of employment protection legislation, the presence of minimum wages and the coverage of union contracts in the workforce; all these aspects tend to be grouped together in the concept of labour market institutions. Stronger institutions have an egalitarian effect on wage disparities; in recent decades the weakening of such labour market institutions has been associated with rising inequalities among wage earners (Salverda and Checchi, 2014).

It is remarkable that the last OECD report on inequality (OECD, 2015) emphasises the responsibility of weaker labour market institutions in the rise of wage inequality and argues for a reversal of policies. The report acknowledges that 'previous analysis has shown that declining union coverage had a disequalising effect on the wage distribution' and that 'high union density and bargaining coverage, and the centralisation/co-ordination of wage bargaining tend to go hand in hand with lower overall wage inequality in both OECD countries and emerging economies' (OECD, 2015: 42; see also OECD, 2011). Specific attention is devoted to the rise of non-standard jobs that 'can also be associated with precariousness and poorer labour conditions', lacking 'employment protection, safeguards and fringe benefits enjoyed by colleagues on standard work contracts'; the consequences are that:

> A non-standard job typically pays less than traditional permanent work ... These earning gaps are especially wide among low-skill, low-paid workers: non-standard workers in the bottom 40% of earners typically suffer wage penalties of 20% ... Non-standard workers also face higher levels of insecurity in terms of the probability of job loss and unemployment and, in the case of temporary workers, report significantly higher job strain.
>
> *(OECD, 2015: 31)*

The OECD – alongside other major international organisations – has long asked governments to introduce labour market 'reforms' going in the direction of more flexibility, lower employment protection and union power – all policies that have contributed to increase inequality. In an interesting reversal, the OECD – with a view to reducing inequality – now advocates a minimum wage that 'can help supporting low-wage workers and low-income families while avoiding significant job losses' (2015: 42), asks for 'improving social dialogue and industrial relations' and argues that 'addressing labour market segmentation and more balanced employment protection are also important elements of enhancing job quality and tackling inequality' (2015: 43).

In the same vein, a recent IMF study on advanced countries shows that a decline in organised labour institutions is associated with higher inequality measured by Gini coefficients, 'likely reflecting the fact that labor market flexibility benefits the rich and reduces the bargaining power of lower-income workers' (Dabla-Norris *et al.*, 2015: 26). Additional evidence shows that 'more lax hiring and firing regulations, lower minimum wages relative to the median wage, and less prevalent collective bargaining and trade unions are associated to higher market inequality' (Dabla-Norris *et al.*, 2015: 26).

Advanced countries, however, do not seem to pay attention to such advice from the OECD and the IMF; in fact the labour reforms currently introduced in Italy, France and other countries go in the direction of precarisation of labour and reduced employment protection.[9] A reversal of the weakening of labour will have to come from a new ability of workers to organise and obtain better wages and working conditions. As Piketty argued, 'the history of income distribution is always a deeply political history that cannot be reduced to purely economic mechanisms' (2013: 47); the degree of inequality in a society directly depends on the power relations between capital and labour.

Technological change

The changing forms of the power of capital over labour have been deeply shaped by changes in technology. In advanced countries, the last three decades have been characterised by the emergence of the new techno-economic paradigm based on information and communication technologies (ICTs), with a growing role played by the production and use of knowledge, by R&D and innovation and by the diffusion of new organisational forms (Freeman and Louçã, 2001). This has led to the decline of old industries – often with a workforce of medium-skilled, unionised workers – and the emergence of new industries and firms with high opportunities for Schumpeterian profits associated with temporary monopolies as a result of technological advantages.

The rising inequalities in jobs and wages have been investigated by a large literature within the economic mainstream suggesting that *skill biased technical change* is the main explanation (Acemoglu, 2002). The argument is that the diffusion of ICTs has led to an upskilling of employees – measured by the ratio of white- to blue-collar workers, or years of education – and to higher wages for the workers with skills that are complementary to the new technologies (and therefore increase workers' productivity).

This interpretation rests on the idea that wage dispersion is rooted in technological change at the firm level, as innovative firms substitute low-skill workers with high-education, high-wage workers whose competences are complementary to ICTs. The mechanistic view of technology and its effects is a major limitation of this approach; all innovations are assumed to be incorporated in physical capital and are expected to be complementary to high skills. As a consequence, both the high-skill/low-skill employment ratio and the wage premium associated with high skills are expected to increase, and are considered as the sole drivers of higher wage inequality. As argued by Nascia and Pianta (2009), the key process in advanced countries is not technology-driven upskilling, but rather a polarisation of jobs and wages on the base of skills. In recent years, even mainstream approaches have acknowledged the polarisation of jobs, often on the ground of a task-based approach (Autor *et al.*, 2006; Goos and Manning, 2007; Acemoglu and Autor, 2010; Goos *et al.*, 2014), but a deeper understanding is needed of the diversity of patterns of technological change and of their consequences on wages and inequality.

Changes in technology – together with those in labour relations and international production – are indeed affecting the evolution of jobs, skills and wages, but in ways less deterministic than those argued by the *skill biased technical change* view. Building on evolutionary perspectives, we can argue, instead, that technological change is highly uneven across industries and it is important to distinguish between strategies of *technological competitiveness* based on new products, and of *cost competitiveness* based on new processes, considering their different effects on jobs, skills, wages and profits. A few studies have examined the operation of these mechanisms in Europe.

In investigating the *skill composition of employment,* the idea of a general upskilling of the workforce does not stand closer scrutiny. When the white-collar/blue-collar ratio or the high/low education ratio are replaced by data on employees broken down in the main professional groups – managers, professionals, technicians, clerks, craft workers and manual workers – a pattern of polarisation emerges. A study of 36 manufacturing and service industries for the five largest EU countries shows that, in the period of expansion between 2002 and 2007, job creation is found for managers (+3.5 per cent per year) and manual workers (less than 1 per cent per year) only, while job losses affect clerks and skilled manual workers. Such polarising dynamics are particularly strong in services where most job creation takes place. Between 2007 and 2011, when the crisis hit, job losses were huge among blue collars (close to -6 per cent per year), modest among clerks and stable for managers (Cirillo *et al.*, 2014). The explanation of such dynamics is rooted in the different technological strategies of industries. Product innovation and high education lead to more jobs for the highest skills; cost competitiveness and process innovation strategies destroy jobs for clerks and craft workers; and manual workers may increase mainly as a result of growing demand (Cirillo *et al.*, 2014).

Given these dynamics of job polarisation, what happens to wages? Differences among technologies again emerge as an important factor, alongside the usual factors such as education, skills and use of ICTs. A study at the industry level, covering 10 manufacturing and service sectors in seven European countries (Croci Angelini *et al.*, 2009) has found that a higher wage polarisation is found within industries with strong product innovation, a fast employment dynamic and high shares of workers with university education; sectors with greater opportunities for expanding markets and jobs are likely to show increasing wage inequalities, as managers and high-skill workers can obtain part of the rents from innovation. Conversely, wage compression is typical of industries characterised by the diffusion of new process technologies and high shares of workers with secondary education who can increase their competences and productivity by working on new machinery, thereby obtaining higher relative wages (usually in a context of relatively high unionisation and labour market regulation), leading to reduced wage disparities.

Is technology also affecting the functional distribution of income between profits and wages? An investigation on the dynamics of profits and wages in manufacturing industries, covering 10 European countries in the period 1994–2001 (Pianta and Tancioni, 2008), has shown that the real growth of wages per employee was less than half that of total profits. In high innovation sectors, profits increased by close to 8 per cent a year, three times as fast as wages. In low innovation industries growth in profits was 3.5 per cent, again more than twice that of wages. The parallel explanations of profit and wage dynamics show that the distributional conflict is a strong factor in the evolution of incomes and that both profits and wages grow on the basis of increases in labour productivity. Wages tend to grow faster in the sectors where innovation expenditure (largely because of wages for high-skill researchers) is higher, while profits are driven both by the importance of new products and market power, and by restructuring through the diffusion of new processes and wage-depressing job reductions. The lesson of such evidence is that technological change has the general effect of favouring profits over wages. Profits increase through separate mechanisms in industries relying on technological or cost competitiveness. Conversely, wages grow only when innovation is associated to higher skills of labour; the result is greater inequality rooted in the functional distribution of income (Pianta and Tancioni, 2008).

Technological change is indeed an important mechanism in shaping inequalities, but the above evidence shows that there is no mechanistic effect on jobs and wages. The choice on the direction of innovation depends on the opportunities that are available to industries and on the strategies pursued by firms that are closely linked to the search for greater control over labour. Different technological strategies have different effects on the distribution between profits and wages, and on inequalities among employees in terms of jobs, skills and wages.

International production

The increasing international openness of economies – with greater flows of trade, knowledge and investment – is a major mechanism affecting the dynamics of wages and profits as well as inequalities among employees. We have already seen in the section on the rise of finance how important the opening up of international capital flows has been for the financial expansion of the last three decades. In this section we focus on the specific type of globalisation that concerns the international organisation of production.

A large literature has shown that in advanced countries the relocation of production abroad (or even the threat of relocation) has depressed domestic wage dynamics, especially for blue collars and low-skilled white-collar workers (Feenstra and Hanson, 2003). In the new system of international production, firms tend to maintain in advanced countries highly skilled activities of management, R&D and finance, with relatively few highly paid employees, while reducing jobs and wages for medium- and low-skilled office and factory workers, whose jobs are more likely to be transferred to low-wage developing countries. The outcome in rich countries is a rise in wage inequality and greater polarisation of jobs and skills. Recent studies have focused on the strategies of offshoring parts of production to low-wage countries (or to countries with lower environmental regulations, labour rights, union power, etc.), resulting in complex global value chains where the final value added of goods comes from the fragmentation of production in several countries. Such offshoring strategies are often designed with the explicit purpose of reducing wage costs, leading to higher profit shares (Milberg and Winkler, 2013).

The global distribution between profits and wages is affected by several mechanisms. Freeman (2009) argued that globalisation has doubled the labour force available in the world economy and lowered the overall capital/labour ratio, leading to a greater (relative) scarcity of capital and resulting in higher profits and lower wages. The same analysis has shown that increasing trade, greater openness of national economies and tariff reductions are likely to contribute to greater income inequalities within countries (Freeman, 2009).

Moreover, the effects of technology and international integration on employment and wages are closely connected, as firms facing international competition introduce more innovations and more innovative firms have a competitive advantage in foreign markets. A study comparing the effects of technology and trade on the reduction of low-skilled workers – in the case of US industries in the 1990s – found that the impact of innovation was dominant, while international trade appeared to play a minor role (Berman *et al.*, 1998).

Again, the ability to organise production on an international scale has strengthened the control of capital over labour, and the combined effect of these two mechanisms has reduced jobs, weakened unions, lowered wages and increased inequalities.

Building on the framework summarised in Figure 4.2, we have been able to show how important the power of capital has been in setting in motion four major processes – the rise of finance, control over labour, technological change and international production – that have reshaped capitalism and have resulted in greater profits and financial rents, lower wages, greater disparities among workers and higher overall inequality.

4.5 Oligarch capitalism

The second engine of inequality we identified in chapter 1 is the rise of oligarch capitalism, where a limited number of people concentrate a large and increasing share of income and wealth, and societies are exposed to their economic power and political influence. The economic and policy-related mechanisms that have skewed the distribution of income in favour of the richest individuals require specific studies on the variety of factors that have affected such outcomes.

We have already seen in chapter 2 that in advanced countries a major part of today's inequality is due to the fast rise of top incomes – those of the richest 1 per cent or 5 per cent of the population – that result from a combination of income sources (Atkinson and Piketty, 2007; Alvaredo *et al.*, 2013; Franzini and Raitano, forthcoming).

The richest individuals have benefitted from the rise of the share of profits in national income and from the exceptionally high financial rents fuelled by speculative gains in increasingly complex (and fragile) financial markets. At the same time, traditional national policies that had contained the rise of top incomes have been removed: inheritance taxes have been cancelled or greatly reduced in most countries; the progressive nature of income taxes has been reduced and tax rates on top incomes have been cut everywhere; tax loopholes have been granted to firms and rich individuals. The liberalisation of international financial flows – and the lack of fiscal harmonisation, even in Europe – has also contributed to this outcome, with increasing opportunities for the rich to report their incomes in tax havens with minimal tax rates.

But there is more to it. Within 'wage' incomes an unprecedentedly high compensation has gone to top managers and 'superstars' in selected professions – lawyers, architects, media, entertainment and sport stars. The composition of top incomes by source of earnings has changed. While in the past they came almost exclusively from capital and rents, in recent decades the broadly defined share of labour compensation has increased. In the top 0.1 per cent of incomes in the US the share of income coming from labour has gone up from 20 per cent in the 1970s to around 45 per cent today (Alvaredo et al., 2013). In Italy, for the top 1 per cent the share of labour incomes (from employment and self-employment) rose from 46 to 71 per cent (Alvaredo and Pisano, 2010).

An explanation of these developments has come from Rosen (1981) who has argued that superstar compensation is the result of two factors. First, in a number of markets demand is concentrated on those who are considered to be the best in their field (i.e. the superstars). Second, technological development allows superstars to satisfy, at no additional cost, an ever increasing share of the market (as with global television coverage of major sport events). Along similar lines, Frank and Cook (1995: 109) talked of a 'winner-takes-all society' where one individual can cover (almost) the whole market at the expense of all competitors. Explanations like this convey the idea that super-incomes accrue to those who have won an extremely competitive race; they acknowledge, however, that limited differences in abilities, talents and human capital can result in disproportionate differences in income earned, mirroring what happens in a sport race where there is only one winner.

Such an outcome is rather distant from what we could expect from markets where individuals are compensated on the basis of their productivity – resulting from their talents, education and abilities. Proportionality between productivity and compensation is a characteristic of competitive markets; therefore, the argument that super-incomes are earned in extremely competitive markets seems unwarranted (Franzini et al., 2014). In fact, in many instances power rather than competition is the driving force of such extreme distributional outcomes. Power can provide the ability to protect and enlarge one's own compensation at the expense of others; this allows one to reap rents and is a major explanation of the spiralling compensations of top managers. Power can convince the market about who is the best performer in a particular activity. Finally, power can prevent changes in the property rights regime that would lead to a different distribution of incomes among all those who have contributed to create the value which is behind such incomes.

Oligarch capitalism appears, in fact, as the product of power and privilege. Power and privilege shape the distribution of income and wealth and lead to extreme and unacceptable inequalities. As pointed out in chapter 3, such extreme inequalities are reproduced across generations through the inheritance of wealth, which is now shaping to a very large extent access to wealth in advanced countries. The results are drastically reduced opportunities for social mobility and a consolidation of oligarch power. For all these reasons, power and privilege have to be checked, weakened and reduced through appropriate institutional changes and policies if we want to prevent the extreme inequalities associated to a concentration of income and wealth similar to the one typical of a century ago.

We have not addressed in this book the illegal behaviours that may create extreme wealth through criminal activities or corruption in private and public decision making. The power of oligarchs in many countries, however, is often linked to such practices. We can just mention here the studies that have linked inequality and corruption (Uslaner, 2008) and the political connections that are at the root of the fortunes of many millionaires – what has been called 'crony capitalism'.[10] A greater use of political influence, widespread corruption and a blurring of the boundaries between legal and illegal actions may indeed be an emerging – and deeply worrying – characteristic of oligarch capitalism.

4.6 The individualisation of economic and social conditions

The third engine of inequality we identified in chapter 1 is the individualisation of economic and social conditions. This is a process that operates at multiple levels. In cultural terms it includes a breakdown of collective identities, such as those of the middle class and of the working class, that were an important cultural factor in the post-war decades up to 1980 marked by decreasing inequality. In social terms we have experienced a greater complexity of the class structure, with a rise of gender, ethnic, migration and generational factors that have deeply fragmented the social landscape of advanced countries. In economic terms, an individual's income has become more uncertain and less predictable. A greater diversity of employment contracts has emerged, leading to equal jobs with different pay and security. The level of education is not anymore a strong predictor of wage disparities, and a greater role of family background has emerged. In terms of gender, the larger presence of women in employment has introduced deep changes, while in most activities discrimination and glass ceiling effects persist. In generational terms, the employment and income prospects for today's youth are significantly worse than those of a generation ago. Changes in household structure – with smaller families and couples increasingly coming from similar income groups – mean that the same income distribution among individuals may lead to greater disparities at the household level. Finally, the increasing importance of wealth and inheritance means that standards of living – at the top of the distribution, but also for the 'patrimonial middle class' – may be affected by returns to wealth more than by income flows.

In this section we cannot investigate all these multiple dimensions, but it is safe to argue that all such factors have contributed to rising disparities within wage earners; they have also weakened the ability of the 'bottom 90 per cent' to resist the rise of the 'top 10 per cent', resulting in higher overall inequality. We focus here on the fragmentation of employment conditions and on the role of education and family background. We have already seen in section 4.4 other ways in which the power of capital has been able to fragment and control labour.

Unequal conditions

The most immediate sign of individualisation of economic conditions is the decline of standard employment – full-time, permanent jobs with union contracts, employment protection, social insurance and pension systems. The 2015 ILO report has documented the rise of non-standard jobs and has showed that 'over 6 out of 10 wage and salaried workers worldwide are in either part-time or temporary forms of wage and salaried employment. Women are disproportionately represented among those in temporary and part-time forms of wage and salaried employment' (ILO, 2015: 13).

We have already seen that such developments have led to lower wages and greater disparities. But there are also longer-term effects of such fragmentation of employment contracts. The ILO report emphasises that non-standard workers generally are not covered by existing employment protection rules and social protection systems, including unemployment benefits and pensions. Both have been designed for standard employees and in most countries have not been adjusted to include the needs of non-standard workers, most of whom are women (ILO, 2015: 14). In this way, a more individualised, non-standard employment condition is likely to have a lasting effect on lifetime incomes and pensions, expanding disparities at the bottom of the distribution.

What about the generational divide? Much of the above evidence has pointed out that the youth are disproportionally represented in non-standard employment and have dimmer prospects for obtaining income and wealth compared with the previous generation. This does not mean, however, that the divide between old and youth is going to shape inequality in our society. Piketty argues that 'the rise of human capital and the replacement of class war by age war are in large part illusions' (Piketty, 2013: 49). The divisions in terms of income and wealth between households at the top and at the bottom of the distribution remains crucial, and there is no base for presenting our aging societies as characterised by a new fundamental divide between equally privileged old people and equally discriminated youth.

Education and family background

In his book, Piketty argues that, facing the dangerous rise of inequality, 'the main force of convergence is the diffusion of knowledge and the investment in education that is essentially a non market mechanism – knowledge being a typical public good' (Piketty, 2013: 47–8). Can education in fact be the answer to inequality?

Mainstream approaches argue that education is a major determinant of workers' productivity and earnings, in a view that is coherent with both market efficiency and equality of opportunities. An increase in wage inequalities – so goes the argument – simply reflects the higher productivity and compensation of workers with the highest human capital or education.

In chapter 2 we have seen that research on European countries has found, instead, that education plays a modest role in the mechanisms behind wage inequality; only 20 per cent of wage disparities are due to differences in education, while the rest is because of inequality within groups of workers with the same education (Franzini and Raitano, forthcoming).

The explanation of such diversity in labour incomes given the same educational attainment can be found in three types of factors: the 'structural' specificities of workers' jobs, the types of labour contracts and labour markets conditions and the 'personal' (and family-related) characteristics of individual workers. The former reflect the strong differences across industries and firms in terms of knowledge, R&D, nature of innovation and market power that result in workers' productivity and end up in earning disparities. The second factor – with an increasingly important role – is related to workers' labour contracts. In Europe employees with tertiary education, but with a temporary or part-time contract, have a considerable probability of ending up in the lowest part of the distribution of income. The third factor points out the role of competences and opportunities acquired not through an education accessible to all, but rather from the family background of individuals; a number of studies have shown that the education and profession of parents are key determinants of the educational attainments and earnings of sons and daughters. In most cases, the influence of the family of origin is stronger than educational levels in predicting individuals' incomes (Franzini *et al.*, 2013).

In chapter 3 we have seen how important the family background can be in determining individuals' life chances, educational attainments and earned wages. Several studies – ranging from economics to psychology – offer good but partial explanations of this influence. In particular, economic models stress the importance of human capital, which is considered both a crucial determinant of individual earnings and a variable on which family conditions exert a major influence.

The approach of the economic mainstream – rooted in the 'the family investment theory' of Becker and Tomes (1979) – states that a family's income and wealth are the key means for investing in human capital in the presence of imperfect capital markets. It is assumed that individual earnings depend on the human capital acquired through education, and that the latter depends on the family's income. Empirical evidence, however, shows that in advanced countries income disparities across generations are highly related to current inequalities, showing a persistence – rooted in family wealth, privilege and networks of connections – stronger than the one expected by the advocates of social mobility through 'equal opportunities' and market processes. The countries with higher current inequality seem to be the same as where the inter-generational transmission of inequality is higher.

When we investigate the individualisation of economic and social conditions, it is important to consider not only the fragmentation of workers in the labour market in terms of education, skills and wages, but also the relevance of family backgrounds – and in particular the network of social contacts and the soft skills acquired (shown in chapter 3) – in shaping wage disparities and in reproducing unacceptable inequalities across generations.

4.7 The retreat of politics

Finally, the fourth fundamental mechanism at the root of today's inequality is the retreat of politics. The next chapter addresses the need for political action on inequality and proposes a set of policies that could reduce disparities. In this section we can simply point out the ways that public policies could affect the distribution of income and wealth and the resulting inequalities – as shown in Figure 4.2.

Inequalities in terms of disposable income and living standards are the results of State actions that can mitigate the outcomes of market processes. As we have seen in chapter 2, governments can act to reduce inequalities through taxation, social transfers and the provision of in-kind services. National experiences widely differ, according to welfare regimes. Public social spending ranges from about 25 per cent of GDP in Nordic and Continental Europe to 19 per cent in Anglo-Saxon countries, where a high share of transfers (43 per cent) are targeted to the bottom quintile of income earners. While there are difficulties in assessing the impact of in-kind transfers, we have seen in Figure 2.9 that advanced countries are able to reduce significantly disparities through such policies. Additional estimates of the reduction in inequality through the presence of public services – in particular universal access to education and health – suggest that the average reduction of the Gini coefficient on disposable income is 37 per cent in countries of the Nordic welfare regime and 24 per cent in both the Anglo-Saxon and Continental Europe groups (where Italy and Spain are included) (Esping-Andersen and Myles, 2009).

However, when we look at the health conditions of citizens, even the best European welfare states appear to have failed to reduce inequality of life expectancy, as the prospects for the poor have substantially worsened in many countries. Conversely, in advanced countries major egalitarian improvements have been achieved in the 'existential' dimension, reducing inequalities associated to status, gender, ethnicity and other social characteristics (Therborn, 2013: ch. 8).

The possibilities of redistribution, however, have been constrained by the operation of the other engines of inequality investigated in this chapter. The rise of finance and the larger share of profits have been able – to some extent – to escape taxation thanks to their international mobility and the use of fiscal havens. With stagnant wages (already paying relatively high tax rates), and slow overall GDP growth, the flow of public resources available for redistribution has not expanded. Moreover, in the last decades policy changes have directly weakened the extent and the effectiveness of redistribution. The less progressive taxation on income, low taxes on finance and wealth and the reduction or cancellation of inheritance taxes have favoured the rich and increased disparities in disposable income. After the 2008 crisis, especially in Europe, austerity-inspired limits to public deficits and debt, reduced taxation, privatisation of services and reduction of social provisions were introduced. They were expected to help restart growth and have had the opposite result – a prolonged stagnation, with further increases in overall inequality.

But public policy has not been confined to redistribution alone. In the last three decades liberalisation, deregulation and privatisation have been at the centre of government action in all advanced countries, strengthening the other mechanisms of inequality investigated above. What we need to understand, therefore, is the overall role that the retreat of politics has played in shaping a more unequal economy and society. And how a return of egalitarian, democratic politics – with a range of appropriate policy actions – could help reverse the extreme inequality we face today. These are the questions of our final chapter.

Notes

1   The rate of return on capital 'measures the yield on capital over the course of a year regardless of its legal form (profits, rents, dividends, interest, royalties, capital gains, etc.) expressed as a percentage of the value of capital invested', it is therefore a broader concept than the 'rate of profit' and much broader than 'the rate of interest', while incorporating both (Piketty, 2013: 93).

2   Rough estimates at the world level suggest a stability of the returns to capital between 4 and 6 per cent, while in the period of most rapid growth (1950–2012) the world economy expanded by less than 4 per cent per year. However, when we consider the returns to capital net of taxes, estimates suggest that they fell to 1 per cent in the 1913–1950 period, returning to just above 3 per cent in 1959–2012 – in both cases the growth rate of the economy has been higher than returns to capital (Piketty, 2013: 562–5, Graphs 10.9 and 10.10). If we consider the rates of return net of taxes for advanced countries, the r > g gap is likely to be reduced.

3   This issue has been raised also by Solow (2014), Real-World Economics Review (2014), Rognlie, (2015), Weil (2015), Wade (2014) and Galbraith (2014). According to the latter, 'Piketty wants to provide a theory relevant to growth, which requires physical capital as its input. And yet he deploys an empirical measure that is unrelated to productive physical capital and whose dollar value depends, in part, on the return on capital' (Galbraith, 2014). Galbraith – in the footsteps of Marx – also argues that Piketty forgets that capital is a social relation: 'the essence of capital was neither physical nor financial. It was the power that capital gave to capitalists, namely the authority to make decisions and to extract surplus from the worker' (2014; in the same vein see also Lordon, 2015).

4   A more specific controversy has concerned Piketty's wealth data. In 2014 the *Financial Times* and the *Wall Street Journal* published articles arguing that his data on rising wealth inequality in the US and Europe were distorted by problems of estimation at the top of the distribution. The method used by Piketty, however, makes appropriate adjustments and his findings have resisted such criticism. The main problem with wealth data, in particular for the very rich, is because of tax havens, and further studies have explored this issue (Zucman, 2014). However, a reasonable assumption is that tax havens induce an underestimation of wealth concentration. This is particularly true for Europe as there is substantial evidence that a large part of the assets hosted in tax havens come from the rich of European countries.

5   The classic growth model is that of Solow (1956); the historical perspective and data on long-term growth are drawn from Maddison (2007); on the recent debate on growth slowdown see Gordon (2014).

6   In order to obtain the share of capital in national income we can multiply the rate of return on capital by the capital/income ratio. With a rate of return around 5 per cent and a capital/income ratio equal to six, the capital share is 30 per cent.

7   Piketty writes that 'r>g does not in itself imply anything about wealth inequality'; 'for a given structure of shocks, the long run magnitude of wealth inequality will tend to be magnified if the gap r–g is higher' (Piketty, 2015: 73, 75).

8   A classical view on how changes in capital–labour relations resulting from high employment affect capital's investment decisions and business cycles is in Kalecki (1943). A global perspective on the long-term evolution of the conditions of labour is in Silver (2003); the impact of globalisation on labour and inequality is examined in Freeman (2009). The ILO reports on wages and employment (ILO, 2014, 2015) document the key dimensions of the current weakening of labour in terms of falling wage shares and precarisation of jobs. The qualitative dimension of work in Europe is explored in Eurofound (2015b).

9   In Italy the government introduced in 2014–15 the Jobs Act, with wide-ranging reforms reducing employment protection. A critical analysis is in Sbilanciamoci! (2015).

10 A report by *The Economist* ('Planet plutocrats', 15 March 2014) considered a set of industries highly affected by corruption – including oil, gas, chemicals, coal, mining, defence, real estate, ports and airports and telecommunications – and ranked countries on the basis of the ratio between billionaires' wealth coming from such 'crony sectors' and GDP. Hong Kong, Russia and Malaysia were at the top of the list; the UK, the US and France ranked at numbers 15, 17 and 20.

5

POLICIES FOR A MORE EQUAL SOCIETY

5.1 Introduction

Economic inequality, with the magnitude and characteristics documented in the previous chapters, is the result of the four engines of inequality that operate in advanced countries. The fourth mechanism – the retreat of politics – has made possible the unleashing of the other ones through a systematic reduction of the ability of policies to limit and compensate for unequal incomes and wealth.

In the last 30 years politics has retreated in all fields. The power of capital over labour – our first engine of inequality – has been extended in several ways. First, capital has been strengthened by freeing capital flows. Liberalisation and deregulation have allowed the rise of finance, the inflation of asset values through speculative bubbles, greater market power and positions of rent, resulting in the expansion of top incomes and wealth. Privatisations have extended market relations and their unequal outcomes in areas – including public services – that were previously delivering services on the basis of equal social rights, not of unequal ability to pay.

Second, labour has been weakened through trade, investment and innovation policies that have allowed production to be organised at an international scale, with extensive labour-saving new technologies, undermining workers' jobs and wages in advanced countries. Labour has been weakened also by reducing the power of trade unions and employment protection legislation, by creating non-standard employment with multiple labour contracts with poorer wages and workers' protection, and by allowing a reduced coverage of national labour contracts and an increasing fragmentation of earnings. With such changed rules, capital has been able to take away from labour 10 to 15 percentage points of national income, and the labour market has become a place where greater disparities have also been created among wage earners.[1]

Third, within Europe in particular, policies of capital and trade liberalisation have resulted in greater disparities across industries and regions – in terms of economic activity, employment and wages – as a result of a higher concentration of production and market power. After the 2008 crisis in particular, a dynamic of divergence has set in with capital – financial centres, some large banks and larger firms – becoming stronger, labour becoming weaker and national imbalances increasing. In Europe as a whole, this results in a further extension of inequality in market outcomes and income distribution.

The rise of oligarch capitalism – our second engine of inequality – is a direct result of specific policy decisions. The power of top managers and the rise of top incomes, the positions of rent, the greater importance of wealth and inheritance have all resulted from policy decisions, and in particular from tax policies that have allowed high incomes, profits and financial gains to largely escape national taxation – through lack of harmonisation, fiscal havens, loopholes, etc. Policies in all countries have reduced progressivity of income taxes, limited taxation on wealth and reduced or eliminated inheritance taxes. Reduced public expenditure, in particular for education, has reduced the opportunities for social mobility, leaving a greater role for families in affecting employment and earnings of children. In these ways, the retreat of politics has left the space that has been occupied by the new power of a capitalist élite wide open. Through its money and influence, the élite is able to affect the policy process itself, preventing political change and creating a real danger for democracy. Through its ability to transmit privilege from one generation to the next, today's oligarch capitalism may come to closely resemble the deeply unjust and immobile societies of the early twentieth century.

The individualisation of economic and social conditions – our third engine of inequality – has resulted from the policies discussed above that have weakened and fragmented labour, and from the increasing diversity of household conditions, including the combination of falling incomes and rising real estate values for home owners in the middle of the distribution.

In other words, rising inequality is not the result of unstoppable forces – technology, globalisation and economic change – imposed upon powerless societies. It is a result – direct and indirect – of a specific set of political decisions that in the last 30 years have opened the way to the rise of disparities.

Further evidence of the importance of policy comes from the fact that inequality did not follow the same pace – and has not the same characteristics – in countries that had the same exposure to technological change and globalisation, but acted differently in terms of regulation, privatisation, taxation and redistribution. This suggests that policies and institutions matter.

The rise in inequality, therefore, is associated to a broad range of government policies that include not just the interventions for redistribution, but also decisions on the way markets operate, rewards are distributed and economic activities are carried out – as in the case of privatising services where previously a more equal distribution was granted by public provision. Politics can indeed counter economic inequality, but several types of policies are necessary.

In this chapter we suggest a set of policies that can be effective both in reducing inequality and in making it more acceptable, at least according to widely accepted ideas of social justice and fairness. In making our suggestions we refer to the four engines of inequality identified in chapters 1 and 4, even though the measures we are suggesting do not have a one-to-one correspondence with each of them. We will also distinguish between measures that have an impact through changes in institutions and rules, and purely redistributive measures, acting after market outcomes. Furthermore, some of these measures can be implemented in the short run while others are more structural and can become effective only in a longer time span.

We start with a brief discussion on the broad objectives that a set of policies aimed at reducing inequality should pursue and their importance; we then address specific objectives and the tools that make achieving them possible.

5.2 Why should inequality be reduced?

Suggesting policies against inequality is not the same thing as arguing that complete economic equality should be the ultimate goal of such policies. In the debate on inequality those who stand for not correcting existing inequality very often make the point that a completely egalitarian society could not work and would be unfair. But correcting existing inequality is not the same as advocating a completely egalitarian society. Most people can easily recognise that some forms of income inequality can be fair and can be reasonably associated to specific economic and social factors, and at the same time be convinced that existing inequality is extreme, unjust and dysfunctional to the good working of the economy and society. This is enough to argue that inequality should be reduced, even if no detailed criterion for establishing the exact magnitude of such a reduction is defined.

In the last 30 years the belief that reducing inequality would be bad for growth has been dominant. The argument that inequality is good for growth has had a very strong appeal on most governments, international institutions, policy and opinion makers. They all come to the conclusion that inequality is not a problem, after all. Two elements underpin such a conclusion: the first is that economic growth is a much more important objective, even from an ethical point of view, than equality; the second one is that the positive association between inequality and growth rests on proven evidence.

Both these statements are highly disputable, as many have argued, and most recently Tony Atkinson (Atkinson, 2015). If actually faced with the alternative between less inequality and less economic growth, a society could reasonably choose less inequality. A choice like this is almost ideal for experimenting with the concept of democracy as 'public reason', advocated by Amartya Sen (2009), or for applying deliberative democracy in one form or another. As is well known, deliberative democracy differs from aggregative democracy because it is not only about counting preferences, it is also about motivating preferences and in allowing preferences to be adapted during the deliberative process. All this makes clear a more general point: the choice of the degree and characteristics of inequality should be the result of a truly democratic decision. In our societies we are very far from a serious discussion on these issues.

The second argument – inequality helps growth – is simply not proven. No general link can be identified between the degree of income inequality and GDP growth, as argued by Atkinson (2015: 259, Figure 9.3). For instance, very many countries have a Gini index of around 0.3, and show widely diverging growth rates between 1990 and 2013. Other factors have to be considered, including structural conditions of economies, the institutions at work and the policies adopted (Franzini, 2010; Rodrik, 2014).

On the inequality–growth argument, in fact a major change of views in the mainstream itself is under way, as pointed out in chapter 1. The last OECD report on inequality concludes that:

> When income inequality rises, economic growth falls. The negative effect of inequality on growth is determined by the lower part of the income distribution: not just the poorest decile but the bottom 40% of income earners. Redistribution through income taxes and cash benefits does not necessarily harm growth. Inequality has a negative impact on growth through the channel of human capital: the wider is income inequality, the lower is the chance that low-income households invest in education.
>
> *(OECD, 2015: 60)*

Similar conclusions are reached in an IMF Staff Note (Ostry *et al.*, 2014) assessing the impact of redistribution, i.e. the attempt to reduce inequality by taxing the rich and transferring income to the poor. The study finds no evidence that this is negative for growth; rather, they show that inequality does not lead to faster growth, and only very sharp redistribution measures are negative for growth. The main implication is that we should prevent too high market inequalities from emerging, so that a limited redistribution can lead to a limited inequality in disposable income and a sustained rate of growth.[2] A recent IMF study has documented the contrasting effects on GDP growth of an increase in the income share of the top 20 per cent – resulting in medium-term GDP decline – and of the bottom 20 per cent – resulting in higher GDP growth. It has emphasised the role of fiscal policy in addressing inequality, pointing out the need for 'greater reliance on wealth and property taxes, more progressive income taxation, removing opportunities for tax avoidance and evasion, better targeting of social benefits' and has argued that 'removing tax relief – such as reduced taxation of capital gains, stock options and carried interest – would increase equity and allow a growth-enhancing cut in marginal labor income tax rates' (Dabla-Norris *et al.*, 2015: 30).

However, the effect of inequality on growth, either positive or negative, is not by itself sufficient to establish what to do with inequality. We cannot avoid a direct discussion about how much inequality, and with what characteristics, we can tolerate in our societies.

The inequality resulting from capital–labour relations and from market outcomes is the result of processes that cannot be considered acceptable because of the asymmetries existing among economic actors; in markets not all people have the same starting conditions and, as a consequence, the stronger players obtain higher incomes and profits with no acceptable justification on the basis of widely shared ethical principles. As argued elsewhere (Franzini, 2013), if this is the case at least part of the observed inequality is unacceptable.

It is not easy to say which level of income inequality is the 'fair' one. However, the emerging general consensus – including the views of international organisations such as the OECD (2011, 2015) – is that the present level of inequality is too high, and in conflict with the values shared by a majority of citizens.

Some argue that observed income inequality is the result of processes that preserve equality of opportunity, and therefore this is compatible with such a notion of equity. This belief rests on weak ground, as proved by the evidence – in chapter 3 – that in most countries inequality is highly transmitted from one generation to the next. Moreover, we have seen that the countries with higher current inequality are the same ones where the inter-generational transmission of inequality is higher; this suggests that fighting current inequality may help to make social mobility a more concrete possibility and reduce a particularly disturbing feature of inequality: its persistence.

Moreover, in general, if we accept that inequalities resulting from better conditions for which no merit can be invoked are to a large extent unacceptable, moving in the direction of reducing their influence on economic inequality is to move in the direction of a more acceptable inequality. In the same vein, compensating *ex post* for inequalities because of differences in such initial conditions is a move towards a more acceptable inequality. This implies that redistribution should take, so to speak, from the undeserving rich and give to the deserving poor.

5.3 How can inequality be reduced?

We will now introduce a series of policy proposals based upon the analysis we have carried out in this book. In suggesting them we have in mind the four engines of inequality discussed in chapters 1 and 4 – the power of capital over labour, oligarch capitalism, individualisation and the retreat of politics. As we will explain, not each policy action can be associated to a specific engine, nor does each suggested measure affect one engine only. Policies may affect the overall context of the economic system, the rules and institutions that shape its operation and the specific conditions in which individuals and social groups enter into market relations. The measures we suggest include actions primarily aimed at reducing and modifying market income inequality and measures that redistribute income or wealth *ex post*. Moreover, there is a need for an integrated approach for assessing the impact on inequality of each policy measure taken in a wide variety of fields. As the inequality patterns are differentiated across countries – as seen in chapter 2 – some of the policies proposed are more appropriate for some countries, and other measures are better suited for others. The list of measures we suggest is partial, and many more actions could be proposed in order to reduce inequality directly and indirectly. Those on which we focus are a coherent set of integrated actions, including widely acceptable policies, some of which have been proposed by many international organisations, political forces, social groups and experts. As in all this book, we do not consider the specific policies that are addressed to poverty; we think that a strong policy against inequality is by far the more effective and appropriate road that can bring us to a reduction of poverty too.

The context of the economic system

The analysis of chapter 4 has pointed out the importance of the systemic changes that have transformed capitalism in the last 30 years, including the expansion of finance, globalisation and technological change. Discussing the policy agenda that could address this range of forces is well beyond the scope of this book. However, we should remember that such developments have gone hand in hand with the retreat of politics we identified as an engine of inequality, setting the context in which disparities have increased. Therefore, a positive effect on the reduction of inequality would emerge from a return of public intervention regulating and limiting finance, controlling the process of globalisation and the direction of technological change.[3] Considering the extent of tax evasion and elusion by corporations and rich individuals, moves towards tax harmonisation and a ban on fiscal havens would also have important egalitarian impacts.

The impact of the crisis started in 2008 has been repeatedly pointed out as a factor strengthening inequalities. In most economies – in particular in Eurozone countries – the crisis has been followed by severe austerity policies that have prolonged the recession. We do not address here the macroeconomic policies – fiscal and monetary – that create the context in which growth and distribution take place. We can just point out that excessive fiscal consolidation has lowered growth and in most countries has made distribution more unequal. The expansionary monetary policy – immediately adopted by the Federal Reserve, much later by the ECB – has mainly sustained the value of financial assets, with little effect on real investment, growth and prices, opening the door to a risk of deflation. A higher inflation target – say at 4 per cent – has been proposed (Krugman, 2012) as a way to spur growth and reduce the burden of private and public debt. A higher inflation could indeed reduce the value of financial assets that are mainly owned by the rich and favour debtors – both firms and poorer individuals. However, creditors could demand in turn greater nominal returns for their investments. With high inflation, workers could suffer a loss of real income if wages are not indexed to prices or labour is unable to gain from wage bargaining. Therefore, a higher inflation has uncertain effects on the reduction of inequalities.

We have left outside the scope of our book the question of the environmental sustainability of the economic system. This is a serious factor, generating new types of inequalities in terms of having access to environmental quality, natural resources and escaping the worst consequences of climate change. Policies for reducing climate change and expanding environmental protection should also be seen as conducive to preventing higher inequalities (see Basili *et al.*, 2005).

Rules and institutions for equality

A specific set of policy changes has to address the rewriting of the rules according to which markets operate and the rebuilding of institutions that are more conducive to egalitarian policies and outcomes. The rules to be modified include those shaping market earnings that at present – as we have seen in chapter 3 – lead to outcomes that reflect undeserved advantages or disadvantages, leading to unacceptable inequalities; in other words, there is a need to make markets possibly more 'impartial'.

Laissez-faire approaches typically argue that the rules of the game 'spontaneously' establish themselves in the real world and that they cannot be subject to any kind of evaluation and should not be changed. Such an attitude would actually lead to maintaining the view that individual success or failure is always justified independently from the nature and content of the rules of the game, for instance whether they do or do not allow advantages on the basis of family background or skin colour. This cannot be accepted. The institutions of income distribution are legitimate not because they dispense prizes according to family background, skin colour or other undeserved characteristics, but on the basis of the claim that they value individual characteristics like merit, effort and abilities obtained through procedures everybody can have access to.

Reducing income inequality and redistribution

Market inequality, and in particular inequality in labour earnings, can be reduced in two different ways that are not, however, in conflict with one other. The first way is to reduce inequality in the initial conditions that lead to income inequality; the second one is to introduce redistribution in order to compensate for unequal and unjust outcomes, or to assure access to important social rights for all citizens. Efforts to improve initial conditions should focus on the characteristics – such as education – that the market is supposed to assess when shaping earnings. When introducing taxation as a tool for redistribution, we should remember that, when markets are monopolistic or there is a strong degree of market power, taxes can be translated into higher prices paid by consumers, eluding the expected redistributive effect; this implies that a reduction of inequality cannot rely on taxation alone and several tools have to be used at the same time.

An integrated view of egalitarian policy objectives

Besides the specific measures that are discussed below, however, there is a major novelty that has to be introduced in public debate and in policy processes: an explicit identification of an overarching objective of public action on inequality and recognition that reducing inequality is an effort that has to develop across all fields of policy action. It should require that each policy area – from macroeconomic to industrial policy, from social to environmental policy – explicitly assesses the inequality impact of the measures undertaken. As Joseph Stiglitz argues in his most recent book, 'Inequality is affected by virtually every policy that the government undertakes' (Stiglitz, 2015: 233).

TABLE 5.1   Policies for reducing inequality

---

a. Rebalancing capital–labour relations
Regulation and downsizing of finance
Limiting positions of rent
A fair distribution of the benefits of technology and productivity
An effective minimum wage and greater role of national labour contracts

b. Stopping oligarch capitalism
Controlling top incomes
A high inheritance tax

c. Reducing individualisation of economic conditions
Reducing the fragmentation of employment contracts
Strengthening an egalitarian public education

d. A return to policies of effective redistribution
International and national taxation of wealth
Greater progressivity of personal income tax
A minimum income

Measures proposed are grouped on the basis of their relevance in addressing the four engines of inequality.

This is particularly important in the European context. The EU has established its Europe 2020 strategy in order to chart the desirable future evolution of European economy and society (European Commission, 2010). Dozens of key variables have been identified as policy targets that member countries are forced to achieve – as in fiscal policy restraint – or encouraged to pursue – as in employment, R&D, education or environmental targets. None of them concerns inequality. The blindness of current political process to the inegalitarian consequences of all sorts of policy is striking, and has its roots in the old and now discredited argument that 'inequality does not matter'. National (and European) politics has to identify clear objectives of inequality reduction in a specific time-frame, and develop an integrated process of implementation and assessment that involves all the relevant policies fields.

We consider now a set of specific policy proposals that can have a direct effect of inequality reduction. The summary list is in Table 5.1. We present them under headings that refer to the four engines of inequality discussed in this book – rebalancing capital–labour relations, stopping oligarch capitalism, reducing individualisation of economic conditions and a return of policies for effective redistribution.

a. Rebalancing capital–labour relations

Regulation and downsizing of finance

The regulation of finance is an issue that goes well beyond the agenda of a policy against inequality. It is a question at the heart of the economic system. However, the rise of finance has been a key element in the two engines of inequality we identified – the power of capital over labour and oligarch capitalism. The specific measures in this field – proposed by a very large literature and by authoritative sources – include: a return to a division between commercial and investment banking; a generalised tax on all financial transactions to limit speculative trading; strong limitations on financial derivatives; in the more radical versions, also some regulations on capital movements are proposed.[4]

These measures would have the effect of reducing the rate of return to financial investment and the inflation of financial asset values that is at the core of the rising capital/income ratio, two key sources of rising inequality according to Piketty (2013). In turn, such a downsizing of finance would put less pressure on profit maximisation in firms and leave more room for real investment, higher wages and a more balanced functional distribution of income. Stricter rules on finance would also have the direct effect of preventing the huge enrichment that has been frequent in the last decades through speculative activities. Often such enrichments are the result of the possibility of appropriating very large gains if high-risk investments are successful and dumping on society the losses if they fail, as happened in many cases after the 2008 financial crisis.

Limiting positions of rent

Very high earnings of individuals and firms almost always embody rents that typically result from a lack of effective competition (Stiglitz, 2012). This calls for measures that challenge monopolistic power and enhance competition, in particular in activities characterised by very high returns and earnings. In recent years competition has almost exclusively performed the role of keeping low the lower earnings, rather than challenging higher incomes. Policies should eliminate obstacles to a greater competition, limiting market power and economic privilege. In the case of top earners, policies should reduce barriers to pursue the best jobs, including difficulties in accessing the competences required and new factors, such as notoriety, which very often are not the result of abilities that the market should reward (Franzini et al., 2014).

A fair distribution of the benefits of technology and productivity

Rapid technological change, especially in information and communication technologies, has led to the rise of new markets where huge 'Schumpeterian' profits are made, dominated by firms often with monopoly power. Such developments have often had a strong financial dimension, most of all in the US, with high-risk investments involved and booming stock values of high technology firms. The gains from this have been highly concentrated in top incomes, while the funding of the research that made such innovations possible has largely come from public sources – and the public sector has often had to cover the losses when new projects failed (Mazzucato, 2013a, 2013b). A more balanced distribution of the benefits of technology between public and private interests has been proposed through changes that would assign a greater share of the gains to the public organisations that have shaped the emergence of new technologies and to the workers involved. Tools that have been proposed include granting State institutions shares of the high technology firms benefitting from public R&D; creating and expanding public investment banks that could fund risky projects and obtain the benefits of success; and modifying intellectual property rights rules to emphasise the public dimension of knowledge created through public R&D. Greater resources flowing to public organisations would limit the rise of top incomes and, moreover, provide greater resources for underfunded basic R&D and public education that are essential for the innovation process itself (Lazonick and Mazzucato, 2013; Mazzucato, 2013b; Lazonick, 2015).

A second way technological change has affected income distribution is through the direction taken by innovations. Considering the functional distribution of income, profits have increased much more than wages as a result both of new products that offer temporary monopoly power and of new processes that replace labour. The latter has often the effect of reducing the quantity (and sometimes also the quality) of employment used, weakening labour in its relationship to capital (Pianta and Tancioni, 2008; Nascia and Pianta, 2009; Croci Angelini et al., 2009). Technology and industrial policies could be introduced and expanded in order to orient innovation in a direction that could have less inegalitarian effects, as argued by Atkinson (2015), and expand – rather than replace and reduce – the quality of labour used, especially in services where human activity remains important. Public organisations could directly introduce labour-enhancing innovations; tax incentives and R&D support could primarily go to firms that give priority to new products, rather than new processes; and the fields and missions where resources should go could include ICT applications, environmental sustainability and health and welfare services – labour-intensive activities where labour skills and wages are higher than average.[5]

Technological change is a major driver of productivity growth in firms, which draws from a variety of other factors – increased education, organisational change, better work practices, etc. Considering the wide gap that has opened in the last decades between productivity and wage growth – with the exception of few countries, see chapter 2 – it is important to design better institutional arrangements that may allow productivity increases to be equally shared between capital and labour and among all workers. We should remember that when productivity and wages increase at the same rate – with no changes in external inputs and prices – the relative distribution between profits and wages does not change, and inequality could worsen only if disparities increase within wages (or profits). There is ample room, therefore, for expanding wages to catch up with productivity growth, and doing it in an egalitarian way, if possible, through national collective labour contracts that have been found to be the most effective mechanism for reducing wage inequalities (see below).

An effective minimum wage and greater role of national labour contracts

In the distribution of income between profits and wages, the former have been able to climb to record levels, while the latter have been falling through the floor. It is time to introduce an effective floor that prevents the fall of wages, in particular of the lowest paid. The number of working poor is on the rise in many countries and a legally binding minimum wage could be an effective tool to prevent that. Such a threshold is generally set by legislation – as happens in the US, the UK, Germany and France – or could be the result of national labour contracts that become enforceable for all workers (see Schulten and Müller, 2014).

Mainstream views generally oppose minimum wages, arguing that they would reduce labour demand and result in falling employment of the lowest skilled. Evidence for the UK, however, shows that when the average wage of the workers in the lowest 10 per cent of earnings has increased, no negative impact on employment has emerged (Stewart, 2004; Swaffield, 2012). Likewise, in Germany the gradual introduction at the start of 2015 of a minimum wage of €8.50 – 62 per cent of the median hourly pay – has been associated to expanding employment. The design of the measure is important and its aim should be to raise the lowest wages without undermining the next-to-lowest wages; this is why a close coordination between minimum wages and national labour contracts – with the layers of pay rises on the basis of qualification, seniority, responsibility, etc. – is important.

In turn, a greater role should be returned to national labour contracts negotiated between employers and unions. In the post-war decades of high growth and low inequality they had a key role in multiple ways. Collective bargaining was the main form for obtaining part of the gains from productivity growth and sharing them among all workers; in national negotiations, unions could exercise greater power and obtain better concessions from employers. National contracts compressed wage inequality in the name of solidarity among workers. The generalised wage increase across an industry acted as a spur to firms to invest and innovate in order to keep up productivity growth. In the last three decades, the role of national labour contracts has been seriously eroded by several factors, including the general weakening of trade unions, which have lost members and political influence as a result of job losses, and more aggressive employers' tactics. These include the 'opting out' of a large number of firms – large and small – which refused to grant the agreed wages in many countries, the policy emphasis on the need for flexibility in wages and labour use and the pressure to shift wage bargaining to the firm level on the grounds that this is where productivity increases are obtained and could be distributed efficiently. Without the protection of national labour contracts, without minimum wages (or with standards set at a very low level, as in the US) and with the growing fragmentation of labour contracts and the rise of non-standard employment, workers have been unable to defend their share of national income and disparities among workers have grown substantially (even when we exclude managers). A more acceptable balance of force between labour and capital has now to be restored, and these policies are crucial for giving more strength to labour and for reversing the inequality produced by a falling wage share, by the reduction in real terms of low wages and by the rising disparities within workers' earnings. The proposal for reducing the fragmentation of employment contracts – that contributes to a lower individualisation of economic conditions, as discussed below – is complementary to the above policy proposals.

b. Stopping oligarch capitalism

The emergence of oligarch capitalism is the result of several factors – as we have seen in this book – and is a major engine of the growth of inequalities in advanced countries. There are multiple reasons to oppose it – the need to protect democracy, to have accountability in the exercise of power, opposition to unjustified privilege, the inefficiency that oligarch power brings to the economy, etc. In this section we concentrate on two simple policy proposals that address two major factors that have made oligarch capitalism possible: unrestrained top incomes and lack of inheritance taxes.

Controlling top incomes

In chapter 1 we have seen that in the top 350 US firms the ratio of the compensation of managers to that of average employees rose tenfold from 30:1 in 1978 to 296 to 1 in 2013 (Mishel and Davis, 2014). Conversely, the US President earns 25 times the wage of the worst paid federal employee and even the business 'guru' Peter Drucker has suggested that a 25:1 ratio offers a balanced set of incentives and is conducive to greater efficiency. Clearly, a reduction of top managers' incomes in private firms cannot be legislated and enforced, but several actions can be taken that would make the current behaviour socially unacceptable again. Governments could establish a clear policy for reducing income disparities within firms and organisations, with clear guidelines on acceptable ratios between best paid, average paid and worst paid workers. They could enforce these guidelines within the public sector. They could then state that private firms violating such guidelines will be penalised in access to public procurement, incentives and tax relief, on the ground that extreme disparities burden society with unacceptable social costs that eventually have to be met by public expenditure. This would create incentives within firms – among responsible managers, shareholders, employees and stakeholders – to change the current model of corporate governance that has led to such disparities, introducing – when possible – greater accountability and democracy also in corporate governance. Such actions would not only reduce the compensation of the top 10 per cent – and in particular of the top 1 per cent – but would also deny social legitimation to oligarchs, responding in a highly symbolic way to the widespread popular rejection of the extreme concentration of income, wealth and power in our societies. Similar steps could be taken with the goal of reducing extreme compensations of other top earners – including professionals and entertainment 'stars'.

A high inheritance tax

Inherited wealth is a growing share of total wealth, and is distributed in an extremely unequal way. It is a major factor in the return of our societies to the levels and nature of inequality typical of a century ago and in the emergence of oligarch capitalism. There is a very simple way to prevent all this – the introduction of high, progressive inheritance taxes. The role of taxation of income and wealth is discussed in the next group of policies, concerned with the return of a strong redistribution. Inheritance taxes also have a redistributive role, but they address first of all the unacceptable oligarchic nature of privilege and the reproduction of extreme inequality from one generation to the next. The recent trends towards a reduction or an elimination of inheritance taxes (EY, 2014) should be reversed and a system of taxation should be designed that allows for exemption under a reasonable threshold, that hits the transmission of real estate and financial assets more than productive capital and that prevents the use of fiscal havens or loopholes for evading or eluding taxation. In the discussion of how the tax could be designed, attention should be given to the idea that inheritance could be taxed under a progressive tax on lifetime capital receipts – as Atkinson (2015) suggests – rather than as an upfront payment at the moment of the transfer; attention should also be paid to the incentives on wealth accumulation.

c. Reducing individualisation of economic conditions

Reducing the fragmentation of employment contracts

In all advanced countries the last three decades have seen a proliferation of new employment contracts that differ from the standard of full-time permanent jobs. The recent ILO report (2015) has documented the rise of non-standard employment including part-time, fixed term, temporary and outsourced self-employed jobs, down to forms of apprenticeship and internship that largely involve the youth. Non-standard jobs have been introduced with the justification that greater labour market flexibility was needed, but in fact they are generally associated to very low wages, lack of employment protection and sometimes even a lack of welfare and social rights. This has increased inequality by lowering the wages of the poorer workers and by generally reducing wages of the new generation entering the labour market with such employment contracts.

This segmentation among workers is hardly acceptable; independently from its effects on income inequality, it violates basic social and labour rights and the principle of equal pay for equal work.

Non-standard workers are forced to bear a heavy burden in terms of economic risks and this can easily conflict with efficiency; in most countries the precarisation of employment and life prospects has become a major social problem. Non-standard workers have contributed to deeper inequality in particular in the countries where they are more numerous (Italy, Spain, Ireland and Germany). They often end up in the lower tails of the distribution of income – the so-called working poor. And, most disturbingly, they often have high levels of education, resulting in an actual waste of human capital. Reducing the spectrum of contractual forms is therefore an important policy for contrasting wage inequality and granting basic labour and social rights to all workers. Also, in this case, the measure should be designed in such a way as to prevent negative effects on employment, which could worsen inequality. Finally, this measure would strengthen trade unions in their bargaining with employers, contributing to less unequal capital–labour relations.

Strengthening an egalitarian public education

In chapters 2 and 4 we have seen how important education is for countering the forces of inequality. We have seen that in many countries access to higher education is very much dependent on the economic conditions of the family of origin. This means that the education obtained by the youth tends to mirror economic inequality across families, reproducing disparities from one generation to the next. The obvious policy implication is that public education should be expanded with a clear egalitarian mission – offering all youth more equal opportunities for accessing high-quality, high-wage jobs on the basis of merit and competence, restoring social mobility and increasing in this way productivity and efficiency. Higher numbers of more-educated people would also reduce the positions of rent obtained by top income earners, increasing the competition for the best paid jobs.

Effective measures to counteract this form of unacceptable inequality should be taken through an expansion of public expenditure and quality of services for all levels of education; a reduction of school fees, especially in tertiary education; and with measures for addressing the problem – extremely serious in some countries – of the debt incurred by youth for obtaining higher education. Actions compensating for differences in family background would be more effective if they are attempted from early childhood to correct shortcomings in learning abilities because of disadvantaged family backgrounds.

d. A return to policies of effective redistribution

The retreat of politics has been a major factor in allowing the unprecedented rise of inequality we experience today. In this section we focus on three main policies that could drastically reduce the inequality emerging from market processes through taxation and expenditure. In the case of taxation, a typical argument for reducing tax rates has been that international tax competition would penalise countries with the highest taxation. Moreover, the presence of tax havens would allow for massive elusion of higher taxes. Major efforts clearly need to be devoted to tax harmonisation, in particular within the European Union, and for limiting and controlling transactions in fiscal havens. Still, there is major scope for also implementing, at the national level, tax reforms that can reduce inequality.

International and national taxation of wealth

A progressive global tax on capital is the main policy proposal suggested by Thomas Piketty (2013: chapter 15). As an example, he suggests how the tax rates could be set: 0 per cent on fortunes below €1 million; 1 per cent between €1 million and €5 million; and 2 per cent above €5 million. By applying these tax rates to Europe, revenues equivalent to about 2 per cent of Europe's GDP could be obtained. It is important that all assets are included – real estate, financial assets and business assets – net of debt. Such inclusiveness is a major difference between Piketty's proposal and the taxes on capital already existing in various countries. Most of the latter do not include financial assets and do not take debts into account. Moreover, the tax design should avoid one of the main weaknesses of existing taxes on capital and in particular on real estate: the riddle of exemptions (and the arbitrary rules often adopted for setting the value of real estate), which impair their fairness and lower the revenues they bring in.

A crucial aspect of the tax design is that – except for high levels of wealth – it should make it possible to pay the due amount from the return on assets. Should it not be so (for example, because wealth is of limited magnitude and is not yielding a sufficient monetary return), the owner would be forced to sell his property and this could be unfair to small-wealth owners and could also lead to a backlash against the tax from the not-too-rich. This point has been made, in his critical appraisal of Piketty's book, by Yanis Varoufakis (2014).

Piketty rightly believes that a tax on capital is necessary, alongside a tax on income and on inheritance, in order to counter the 'main force of divergence' – i.e. a rate of return on wealth greater than the growth rate of income – and to stop the increase in wealth inequality. The need for a tax on capital – instead of relying on a more progressive income tax only – comes from the fact that very rich people never declare an income that corresponds to a reasonable rate of return on their wealth. For instance, people owning a fortune of €10 billion usually declare an income less or much less than €10 million. This corresponds to a ridiculous 0.1 per cent rate of return. This is not necessarily on account of tax evasion, but more simply is the result of the common practice of not distributing the whole return to capital, but accumulating the largest part of it in a legal entity created precisely to manage such fortunes (Piketty, 2013: 854). As a consequence, 'income is not a well-defined concept for very wealthy individuals, and only a direct tax on capital can correctly gauge the contributive capacity of the wealthy' (Piketty, 2013: 852). Under these conditions even extremely high tax rates on declared income would not yield revenues that are an adequate share of actual income.

The other characteristic of the tax is that it should be global. The reason is quite obvious in a globalised world. In fact, Piketty argues that the alternative to it would be protectionism, which has many defects among which he includes the dampening of the forces of competition.

Piketty acknowledges that the introduction of such a tax at the global level would require a close international coordination, which is really difficult to achieve in the present conditions and he suggests that it could be initially introduced at the European level. Finally, he makes the important point that 'a tax is always more than a tax: it is also a way of defining norms and categories and imposing a legal framework on economic activity' (2013: 843). In this perspective a further and related advantage of the tax is that everyone would be required to report ownership of capital assets and, as a consequence, international financial transparency would be enhanced.

Piketty's arguments in support of a global capital tax are very strong and this should definitely be part of the policy agenda against inequality. However, there is a need to use the policy space available at the national level without waiting for the appropriate conditions to emerge at the European or global level. Individual countries, especially in Europe, should start introducing a national wealth tax along these lines in the context of tax reforms that could simultaneously reduce taxation on other sources and with the broad aim of maintaining stability in the total tax burden. Again, if some countries are ready to make the first steps in this direction, pressure could mount within Europe for greater attention to the taxation of wealth and for tax harmonisation at the continental level.

Greater progressivity of personal income tax

The most obvious and simple policy instrument available for reducing inequalities is to restore a more progressive taxation on incomes, after three decades in which the tax rates for high incomes have been systematically reduced. A steeper curve for tax rates is required, lowering those at the bottom and raising those at the top, bringing them back to at least 65 per cent – as proposed by Atkinson (2015), who makes a detailed and convincing case for greater progressivity. Other proposals suggest a higher top rate. We can remember that in the UK before the Thatcher government in 1979 the top rate was 83 per cent; in the US the top rate was 91 per cent until 1963, and 70 per cent until 1980. It is also important to revise the complex system of loopholes and deductions that favour higher incomes.

This policy is straightforward because there is very strong evidence that tax reductions for the rich have had negative effects on inequality, but also failed to sustain investment and growth. A simple government decree can change tax rates and there is no need to change methods of tax collection or create new institutions. The political relevance of such a move in a strategy for social justice and equality could be immediately evident and could influence the public debate. Again, such tax changes could be introduced with the broad aim of maintaining stability in the total tax burden; higher taxes on high incomes could be compensated by lower taxes at the bottom of the distribution.

A minimum income

In post-war decades most advanced countries have introduced important redistribution policies as part of the welfare state, including public pensions, unemployment benefits, income support measures, anti-poverty programmes and extensive provision of public services. They have benefitted society as a whole, in particular those at the bottom of the distribution, and have been a major force for the reduction of inequality experienced between 1950 and 1980. In recent decades, however, the importance of social expenditure in public budgets has fallen and frequent changes in welfare systems have reduced the redistributive effects of public action. The result is the fall in household disposable income at the bottom of income distribution, the rise of the working poor and greater inequality because of the falling behind of lower incomes. Moreover, the changes in labour markets, the rise of non-standard employment and the precarisation of work and life prospects have introduced new factors of uncertainty, risk and poverty that need to be addressed by policies.

The most effective way to address such challenges is the introduction of a universal minimum income that could guarantee a dignified standard of living to all citizens as part of their civil and social rights. This would lift the bottom of the income distribution, solve most problems of poverty and reduce inequality. Moreover, this has the important advantage of eliminating the current discriminations among people that may receive different degrees of income support depending on their previous employment contract or work history.

There is a long history of proposals for an unconditional universal basic income, of debates whether public policy should guarantee employment or income and of implications on work ethic, social citizenship, etc. There are merits on both sides of the argument and a reasonable policy could provide in parallel both public jobs and a minimum income.[6] In fact, policies could jointly address guarantees on jobs, on incomes and the measures on the minimum wage in a comprehensive strategy to avoid the presence of the working poor and reduce poverty and disparities. With the present developments in labour markets, the introduction of a minimum income, funded from general taxation, would be an important move forward and simplify national systems of benefits. In fact, each country has developed a specific welfare system to deal with such problems and within Europe major diversities exist. The need for such a measure for the EU as a whole is widely recognised, as proposed by the recent report from Friends of Europe (2015) drafted by a group of distinguished experts holding different views about what a Social Europe could be. Proposals have been advanced for the funding of a minimum income through European funds; this would greatly contribute to reducing disparities in the EU as a whole and to restore the legitimacy of European integration among its citizens.

5.4 The implementation of egalitarian policies

All the policies we advocate tend to interact with one another and have contrasting or reinforcing effects on several variables of relevance for inequality. Therefore, the design of policies in one field has to take into account all the possible complementarities and conflicts arising with other policies; the effects on other elements that are crucial for the success of anti-inequality policies should be carefully evaluated.

In order to avoid a lack of coordination between decision makers on such policies at various levels of government, it is important that each policy be assigned to the more appropriate level of government (local, national or supranational). In this respect, a specific problem in Europe is the balance that has to be found between initiatives at the European Union or at the national levels.

At EU level, a choice has to be made between institutional competition and harmonised policies. As far as inequality (within countries and between countries) is concerned, the need for harmonised policies looks quite strong and the EU should play a crucial role in favouring such policies. In particular, programmes should be designed to meet specific and possibly observable targets – including in the Europe

2020 strategy – and local and national governments should be clearly accountable with respect to them. There is no doubt that the EU should be directly involved and should play a strong role of coordination in almost all the policies we have suggested. This is crucial in the regulation of finance, in the taxing of wealth and incomes and in the need for overall tax harmonisation. The EU role is important also with respect to redistributive measures, reduction of rents and protection of labour. However, in the institutional context of today's Europe, the key initiative will rest with national governments, who have maintained a primary responsibility in these issues.

More generally, in some countries the question of the ability of governments, public administrations and agencies to carry out and implement policies of this type with both efficiency and effectiveness is not obvious, and a lot of attention will have to be devoted to the design and simplification of each measure.

The practical implementation of the suggested policies is hampered by several obstacles. We list the two most important ones, which may also help to explain the huge gap between the statements by politicians on how bad inequality is and the lack of policies introduced to counter it.

The first obstacle is of a cultural and social nature. The level of inequality we observe is also the result of what we can call 'tolerance', or limited aversion to 'inequality'. The reasons why a number of countries exhibit such an attitude are not easy to identify. One reason could be that several people – sometimes those who suffer from inequality – do not know the real extent of disparities and accept inequality as more or less inevitable, perhaps because they cannot identify an effective way to escape from it or because they believe that society is more mobile than it actually is. Another reason is that individuals' limited tolerance to inequality does not find an appropriate political framework – developed either by political forces or social movements – that could turn inequality into a major issue of social and political contention. This involves political economy arguments as well as an analysis of the role of civil societies' organisations in addressing inequality. Allowing this 'voice' to be properly formed and listened to may also help to develop an ethical discourse and democratic deliberation on acceptable inequality and to develop a consensus on the policies that could effectively reduce disparities.

A second and major obstacle is the strength of those who are going to lose from policies aimed at reducing inequality. The issue raises the problem of the links between economic inequality and political inequality, which are one of the major concerns of those who believe that today's inequality – with its specific characteristics of increasing concentration of wealth and income at the top – can endanger democracy and lead to an oligarchic capitalism reminiscent of the *ancien régime* that ruled before the French Revolution. Many scholars have argued that this is a real risk and have produced convincing evidence on how much policies depend on the interests and preferences of the rich or, better, of the very rich (Gilens and Page, 2014; Stiglitz, 2012, 2015; Bartels, 2008). A specific issue in this regard is the funding of political parties and of electoral campaigns. Private funding has become more and more important, even in European countries that previously relied on public funding, and the regulations are becoming more tolerant as different types of limitations (including the maximum individual contribution) are repealed. The consequences of these choices for inequality can be profound and in countries such as the US they are already worrying (Ferguson *et al.*, 2013). In order to overcome these resistances to lower inequality and redistribution, there is a need to mobilise widespread public support for measures that counter forces producing inequality in the market and increase the tax burden on the rich – a development that is still missing in our democracies. A reasonable way to proceed – among others – could be to earmark the revenue from such taxes – in particular the wealth and inheritance taxes – to specific redistributive measures that directly enhance the economic and social wellbeing of most people.

These policies are a coherent package that is capable of addressing the four engines of inequality at the source of today's problems. They act on the deeper processes that generate disparities in the operation of the economic system, they correct the way markets distribute earnings and they assure a fair redistribution through taxation and public expenditure. We have shown in this book that there is overwhelming evidence on the urgency of reducing inequalities, we have clearly identified their sources and the policies we propose offer effective solutions. They are not easy solutions, and complex technical issues need to be dealt with in order to assure a good implementation; a large number of studies, competences and good policy practices are available to this end. Inequality can indeed be reduced through these actions.

What is needed to make this happen, however, is much more than reasonable advice from economists. A strong reversal of inequality – through processes different from the tragedies that brought it down a century ago – can only come from deep social and political change. Society has to stop its tolerance – or even admiration – for the super rich. The connection has to be made between the glittering fortunes of the 1 per cent and the worsening destinies of all the rest. Greed has nothing to do with economic dynamism, and a lot to do with socially dangerous behaviour. The view of unrestrained individualism as an engine of progress has proved to be an illusion; solidarity has to be recognised again as what keeps us together, especially in the times of slow growth that are ahead. A more egalitarian society has to be seen again as a much better society to live in.

Civil society concern and activism is what has kept these ideas alive in the decades of unstoppable disparities. Bottom-up solidarity actions, care and support for the weakest, social justice movements and trade union resistance have shown the direction all society should take; important social mobilisations – although timid, discontinuous and very diverse across countries – have demanded political change.

And yes, political change is what is most important now if we want the rise in inequality to be reversed and its characteristics made more acceptable. Most political parties, parliaments and governments have so far refused to hear the argument that inequality is bad for society as a whole. It is remarkable that this argument is now made by the same international organisations – the OECD and the IMF – that have long preached the virtues of liberalisation, financial expansion and tax cuts for the rich, regardless of their inegalitarian effects. We know that part of the reason is that the rich – large corporations and finance – are increasingly able to influence the political process, with a dangerous corruption of democracy. This makes the fight for equality much more than a question of economic policy. It is a question of fundamental values – clearly stated in most Constitutions of advanced countries. It is a question of making sure that the political process is accountable to social demands – that democracy works in the end. Over inequality, in fact, a major conflict is played out – that of democracy and social justice against the rise of oligarch capitalism.

Notes

1 Jacob Hacker, who was the first to speak of 'pre-distribution' as a necessary strategy along with redistribution against inequality, argued that 'failure to enforce policies supporting workers' organizing rights has undermined labour unions as a force for good pay while corporate governance rules all but asked top executive to drive up their own earnings. Financial deregulation brought great riches for some while crashing the rest of the economy' (Hacker, 2011: 35).
2 Ostry *et al.* (2014) use the Standardized World Income Inequality Database constructed by Solt (2009) that allows long-term comparisons across different countries. A survey of the inequality-growth debate is in Voitchovsky (2009).
3 On the relevance of these issues for policies against inequality see Atkinson (2015, chapter 4). On the broader economic and political context of neoliberalism and the need for a return of politics see Hall *et al.* (2015), Duménil and Lévy (2014) and Marcon and Pianta (2013). On Europe's crisis see Coats (2011), Fazi (2014) and Lehndorff (2015).
4 Effective proposals on regulating finance have come from Aglietta (2014), Economistes Atterrés (2013, 2015), EuroMemo Group (2015), Fazi (2014), Finance Watch (2015) and Lapavitsas (2013).
5 Such policies are presented in Pianta (2014); see the special issue of *Intereconomics* (2015) on policy proposals for a new industrial and innovation policy with articles by Dosi, Cimoli and Stiglitz, Landesmann, Mazzucato, Page, Pianta, Waltz and Cirillo and Guarascio.
6 The case for a basic income is made in particular by Van Parijs and Vanderborght (2005) and by the work of the Basic Income Earth Network (www.basicincome.org). The importance of providing guaranteed jobs as a strategy to reduce inequality has been pointed out by Atkinson (2015: 140). Even the last OECD report on inequality argues that 'direct job creation schemes can serve as a useful back stop to ensure that the long term unemployed and other disadvantaged groups maintain a contact with the labour market' (OECD, 2015: 41).

BIBLIOGRAPHY

Acemoglu, D. (2002). Technical change, inequality and the labor market. *Journal of Economic Literature*, 40, 1: 7–72.

Acemoglu, D. and Autor, D. (2010). Skills, tasks and technologies: Implications for employment and earnings. In Ashenfelter. O. and Card, D. (eds), *Handbook of Labor Economics*, vol. 4B. North Holland, Elsevier, 1,043–171.

Acemoglu, D. and Robinson, J. (2012). *Why Nations Fail. The Origins of Power, Prosperity and Poverty*. New York, Random House.

Aglietta, M. (2014). *Europe. Sortir de la crise et inventer l'avenir*. Paris, Michalon.

Alvaredo, F. and Pisano, E. (2010). Top incomes in Italy 1974–2004. In Atkinson, A. B. and Piketty T. (eds), *Top Incomes over the Twentieth Century. Vol. II: A Global Perspective*. Oxford, Oxford University Press.

Alvaredo, F., Atkinson, A. B., Piketty, T. and Saez, E. (2013). The top 1 percent in international and historical perspective. *Journal of Economic Perspectives*, 27, 3: 3–20.

Anand, S. and Segal, P. (2008). What do we know about global income inequality? *Journal of Economic Literature*, 46, 11: 57–94.

Anand, S. and Segal, P. (2014). The global distribution of income. In Atkinson, A. and Bourguignon, F. (eds), *Handbook of Income Distribution*, vol. 2B. Amsterdam, Elsevier, 937–79.

Armour, P., Burkhauser, R. and Larrimore, J. (2013). Levels and trends in United States income and its distribution. A crosswalk from market income towards a comprehensive Haig–Simons income approach. NBER Working Paper No. 19110. Online, NBER.

Arrighi, G. (1991). World income inequalities and the future of socialism. *New Left Review*, 189: 39–65.

Arrighi, G. (1994). *The long XX Century. Money, Power and the Origins of our Time*. London, Verso.

Arrighi, G. and Silver, B. (1999). *Chaos and Governance in the Modern World System*. Minneapolis, University of Minnesota Press.

Ashenfelter, O. and Card, D. (eds) (2010). *Handbook of Labor Economics*, vol. 4B. North Holland, Elsevier.

Atkinson, A. (2015). *Inequality. What Can be Done?* Cambridge (Mass.), Cambridge University Press.

Atkinson, A. and Bourguignon, F. (eds) (2000). *Handbook on Income Distribution*, vol. 1. Amsterdam, Elsevier.

Atkinson, A. and Bourguignon, F. (eds) (2014a). *Handbook of Income Distribution*, vols 2A and 2B. Amsterdam, Elsevier.

Atkinson, A. and Bourguignon, F. (2014b). Introduction: income distribution today. In *Handbook of Income Distribution*, vol. 2A. Amsterdam, Elsevier, xvii–lxiv.

Atkinson, A. and Piketty, T. (eds) (2007). *Top Incomes Over the Twentieth Century*. Oxford, Oxford University Press.

Atkinson, A. and Piketty, T. (eds) (2010). *Top Incomes, A Global Perspective*. Oxford, Oxford University Press.

Atkinson, A., Piketty, T. and Saez, E. (2011). Top incomes in the long run of history. *Journal of Economic Literature*, 49, 1: 3–71.

Autor, D., Katz, L. and Kearney, M. (2006). *The Polarization of the US Labour Market*, NBER Working Paper No. 11986. Online, NBER.

Bakija, J., Cole, A. and Heim, B. (2012). *Jobs and Income Growth of Top Earners and the Causes of Changing Income Inequality: Evidence from US Tax Return Data*, Working Paper 2012–24. Williamstown (Mass.), Williams College.

Ballarino, G., Braga, M., Bratti, M., Checchi, D., Filippin, A., Fiorio, C., Leonardi, M., Meschi, E. and Scervini, F. (2014). Italy: How labour market policies can foster earnings inequality. In Nolan, B., Salverda, W., Checchi, D., Marx, I., McKnight, A., Tóth, I. and van de Werfhorst H. (eds), *Changing Inequalities and Societal Impacts in Rich Countries: Thirty Countries' Experiences*. Oxford, Oxford University Press.

Bartels, L. M. (2008). *Unequal Democracy. The Political Economy of the New Gilded Age*. New York, Russell Sage Foundation.

Basili, M., Franzini, M. and Vercelli, A. (eds) (2005). *Environment, Inequality and Collective Action*. London, Routledge.

Becker, G. and Tomes, N. (1979). An equilibrium theory of the distribution of income and intergenerational mobility. *Journal of Political Economy*, 87, 6: 1,153–89.

Becker, G. and Tomes, N. (1986). Human capital and the rise and fall of families. *Journal of Labor Economics*, 4, 3: 1–39.

Bell, B. D. and Van Reenen, J. (2013). Extreme wage inequality: Pay at the very top. *American Economic Review: Papers and Proceedings*, 103, 3: 153–7.

Benabou, R. (1996). Equity and effectiveness in human capital investment: The local connection. *Review of Economic Studies*, 63, 2: 237–64.

Berman, E., Bound, J. and Machin, S. (1998). Implications of skill biased technological change: International evidence. *Quarterly Journal of Economics*, 113, 4: 1,245–79.

Bertocchi, G. (2007). *The Vanishing Bequest Tax: The Comparative Evolution of Bequest Taxation in Historical Perspective*, IZA Discussion Paper 2578. Germany and online, Institute for the Study of Labor (IZA).

Birdsall, N., Lustig, N. and McLeod, D. (2011). *Declining Inequality in Latin America: Some Economics, Some Politics*, Working Paper 251. Washington, DC, Center for Global Development.

Björklund, A. and Jäntti, M. (2009). Intergenerational income mobility and the role of family background. In Salverda *et al.* (eds), *The Oxford Handbook of Economic Inequality*. Oxford, Oxford University Press, 491–521.

Björklund, A., Jäntti, M. and Solon, G. (2005). Influences of nature and nurture on earnings variation: A report on a study of various sibling types in Sweden. In Bowles, S., Gintis, H. and Osborne Groves, M. (eds), *Unequal Chances: Family Background and Economic Success*. New York, Russell Sage Foundation.

Blanden, J. (2013). Cross-country rankings in intergenerational mobility: A comparison of approaches from economics and sociology. *Journal of Economic Surveys*, 27, 1: 38–73.

Blank, R. (2011). *Changing Inequality*. Berkeley, University of California Press.

Bogliacino, F. (2009). Poorer workers: the determinants of wage formation in Europe. *International Review of Applied Economics*, 23, 3: 327–43.

Bogliacino, F. and Maestri, V. (2014). Increasing economic inequalities? In Salverda *et al.* (eds), *Changing Inequalities in Rich Countries. Analytical and Comparative Perspectives*. Oxford, Oxford University Press, 15–48.

Bound, J. and Johnson, G. (1992). Changes in the structure of wages in the 1980s: An evaluation of alternative explanations. *American Economic Review*, 82, 3: 371–92.

Bourguignon, F., Morisson, C. (2002). Inequality among world citizens: 1820-1992. *American Economic Review*, 92, 4: 727–44.

Bowles, S. and Gintis, H. (2002). The inheritance of inequality. *Journal of Economic Perspectives*, 16, 3: 3–30.

Bowles, S., Gintis, H. and Osborne Groves, M. (eds) (2008). *Unequal Chances: Family Background and Economic Success*. New York, Russell Sage Foundation.

Brandolini, A. (2005). La disuguaglianza di reddito in Italia nell'ultimo decennio. *Stato e Mercato*, 2: 207–30.

Brandolini, A. (2007). *Measurement of Income Distribution in Supranational Entities: The Case of the European Union*, Temi di discussione 623. Rome, Bank of Italy.

Brandolini, A. and Smeeding, T. (2009). Income inequality in richer and OECD countries. In Salverda *et al.* (eds), *The Oxford Handbook of Economic Inequality*. Oxford, Oxford University Press, 71–101.

Bratsberg, B., Røed, K., Raaum, O., Naylor, R., Jäntti, M., Eriksson, T. and Österbacka, E. (2007). Non-linearities in inter-generational earnings mobility: Consequences for cross-country comparisons. *Economic Journal*, 117: C72–C92.

Braudel, F. (1979). *Civilization and Capitalism, 15th–18th Centuries*. California, University of California Press.

Card, D., Lemieux, T. and Riddel, W. (2003). Unions and wage inequality. *Journal of Labor Research*, 25, 4: 519–59.

Checchi, D. (ed.) (2012). *Disuguaglianze diverse*. Bologna, il Mulino.

Checchi, D. and Garcia-Penalosa, C. (2008). Labour market institutions and income inequality. *Economic Policy*, 56: 600–51.

Checchi, D., Visser, J. and van de Werfhorst, H. G. (2010). Inequality and union membership: The influence of relative earnings and inequality attitudes. *British Journal of Industrial Relations*, 48, 1: 84–108.

Chesnais, F. (ed.) (2004). *La finance mondialisée. Racines sociales et politiques, configuration, conséquences*. Paris, La Découverte.

Cholezas, I. and Tsakloglou, P. (2007). *Earnings Inequality in Europe: Structure and Patterns of Inter-temporal Changes*, IZA Discussion Paper 2636. Germany and online, Institute for the Study of Labor (IZA).

Cirillo, V., Pianta, M. and Nascia, L. (2014). *The Shaping of Skills: Wages, Education, Innovation*, Working Papers in Economics, Mathematics and Statistics 2014/06. Urbino (Italy), University of Urbino Carlo Bo.

Coats, D. (ed.) (2011). *Exiting from the Crisis: Towards a Model of more Equitable and Sustainable Growth*. Brussels, ETUI.

Cobham, A. and Sumner, A. (2013). *Is it all About the Tails? The Palma Measure of Income Inequality*, CGD Working Paper 343. Washington, DC, Center for Global Development.

Corak, M. (2006). *Do Poor Children Become Poor Adults? Lessons from a Cross Country Comparison of Generational Earnings Mobility*, IZA Discussion Paper 1993. Germany and online, Institute for the Study of Labor (IZA).

Corak, M. (2013). Income inequality, equality of opportunity, and intergenerational mobility. *Journal of Economic Perspectives*, 27, 3: 79–102.

Cornia, G. A. (ed.) (2004). *Inequality, Growth and Poverty in an Era of Liberalization and Globalization*. Oxford, Oxford University Press.

Cornia, G.A. (2012). *Inequality Trends and their Determinants*, Working Paper 2012/09. United Helsinki: Nations University World Institute for Development Economics Research (UNU-WIDER).

Croci Angelini, E., Farina, F. and Pianta, M. (2009). Innovation and wage polarisation in European industries. *International Review of Applied Economics*, 23, 4: 309–26.

Dabla-Norris, E., Kochhar, K., Suphaphiphat, N., Ricka, F. and Tsounta, E. (2015). *Causes and Consequences of Income Inequality: A Global Perspective*, IMF Staff Discussion Note. Washington DC, IMF.

Deaton, A. (2005). Measuring poverty in a growing world (or measuring growth in a poor world). *Review of Economics and Statistics*, 87, 1: 1–19.

Di Muzio, T. (2015). *The 1% and the Rest of Us*. London, Zed books.

Di Nardo, J., Fortin, N. M. and Lemieux, T. (1996). Labour market institutions and the distribution of wages, 1973–1992: A semi-parametric approach. *Econometrica*, 64, 5: 1,001–44.

Drezet, V. and Hoang Ngoc, L. (2010). *Il faut faire payer les riches*. Paris, Éditions du Seuil.

Duménil, G. and Lèvy, D. (2014). *La grande bifurcation. En finir avec le néolibéralisme*. Paris, La Découverte.

Economistes Atterrés (2013). *Changer l'Europe!*. Paris, Les Liens qui libèrent.

Economistes Atterrés (2015). *Nouveau manifeste des économistes atterrés*. Paris, Les Liens qui libèrent.

Erikson, R. and Goldthorpe, J. H. (1992). *The Constant Flux: A Study of Class Mobility in Industrial Societies*. Oxford, Clarendon Press.

Ermisch, J., Jäntti, M., Smeeding, T. and Wilson, J. A. (2012). Advantage in comparative perspective. In Ermisch, J., Jäntti, M. and Smeeding, T. (eds), *From Parents to Children. The Intergenerational Transmission of Advantage*. New York, Russell Sage Foundation.

Esping-Andersen, G. and Myles, J. (2009). Economic inequality and the welfare state. In Salverda, *et al.* (eds), *The Oxford Handbook of Economic Inequality*. Oxford, Oxford University Press, 639–64.

Eurofound (2015a). *Recent Developments in the Distribution of Wages in Europe*. Dublin, European Foundation for the improvement of living and working conditions.

Eurofound (2015b). *Eurofound Yearbook 2014. Living and Working in Europe*. Dublin, European Foundation for the improvement of living and working conditions.

EuroMemo Group (2015). What future for the European Union: Stagnation and polarisation or new foundations? *EuroMemorandum 2015*. Berlin, EuroMemo Group.

European Central Bank (ECB) (2013). *The Eurosystem Household Finance and Consumption Survey Results from the First Wave*, Statistics Paper Series, 2. Geneva: ECB.

European Commission (2010). *Europe 2020. A Strategy for Smart, Sustainable and Inclusive Growth*, COM 2020 Final. Brussels, European Commission.

EY (2014). *Worldwide Estate and Inheritance Tax Guide 2014*. London, Ernst & Young.

Farina, F. and Savaglio, E. (eds) (2006). *Inequality and Economic Integration*. London, Routledge.

Fazi, T. (2014). *The Battle for Europe. How an Élite Hijacked a Continent and How We Can Take it Back*. London, Pluto.

Feenstra, R. and Hanson, G. (2003). Global production sharing and rising inequality: A survey of trade and wages. In Choi, E. K. and Harrigan, J. (eds), *Handbook of International Trade*. London: Blackwell.

Ferguson, T., Jorgensen, P. and Chen, J. (2013). Party competition and industrial structure in the 2012 elections: Who's really driving the taxi to the dark side?. *International Journal of Political Economy*, 42, 2: 3–41.

Finance Watch (2015). *Annual Report 2014*. Brussels, Finance Watch.

Fiorio, C., Leonardi, M. and Scervini, F. (2012). La disuguaglianza dei redditi in Italia. In Checchi D. (ed.), *Disuguaglianze diverse*, Bologna, Il Mulino, 137–53.

Fleck, S., Glaser, J. and Sprague, S. (2011). The compensation–productivity gap: A visual essay. *Monthly Labor Review*, January: 57–69. Washington, DC, US Bureau of Labor Statistics.

Forster, M. and Toth, I. (2014). Cross country evidence of the multiple causes of inequality changes in the OECD area. In Atkinson, A. and Bourguignon, F. (eds), *Handbook of Income Distribution*, vol. 2B. Amsterdam, Elsevier, 1,730–836.

Frank, R. and Cook, P. (1995). *The Winner-take-all Society*. New York, Simon and Schuster.

Franzini, M. (2009). Why Europe needs a policy on inequality. *Intereconomics, Review of European Economic Policy*, 44, 6: 328–32.

Franzini, M. (2010). *Ricchi e poveri. L'Italia e le disuguaglianze (in)accettabili*. Milan, Egea.

Franzini, M. (2013). *Disuguaglianze inaccettabili. L'immobilità economica in Italia*. Rome, Laterza.

Franzini, M. and Pianta, M. (eds) (2009). Inequality: Mechanisms and effects. *International Review of Applied Economics*, Special Issue, 23, 3: 233–7.

Franzini, M. and Pianta, M. (2011). *Explaining Inequality in Today's Capitalism*, Working Papers in Economics, Mathematics and Statistics 1108. University of Urbino Carlo Bo.

Franzini, M. and Raitano, M. (2013). Economic inequality and its impact on intergenerational mobility. *Intereconomics: Review of European Economic Policy*, 48, 6: 328–35.

Franzini, M. and Raitano, M. (2014). *Wage Gaps and Human Capital: Looking for an Explanation*. Paper presented at the Progressive Economy Workshop, Brussels, 5–6 March 2014.

Franzini, M. and Raitano, M. (2015). Income inequality in Italy: Tendencies and policy implications. In Sancetta G. and Strangio D. (eds), *Italy in the European Context. Researches in Economics, Business and Environment*. London, Palgrave.

Franzini, M., Raitano, M. and Vona, F. (2013). The channels of inter-generational transmission of inequality: A cross-country comparison. *Rivista Italiana degli Economisti*, 18, 2: 201–26.

Franzini, M., Granaglia, E. and Raitano, M. (2014). *Dobbiamo preoccuparci dei ricchi?* Bologna, Il Mulino.

Fraser, N. (2005). Reframing justice in a globalising world. *New Left Review*, 36: 1–19.

Freeman, R. (2009). Globalisation and inequality. In Salverda *et al.* (eds), *The Oxford Handbook of Economic Inequality*. Oxford, Oxford University Press, 575–98.

Freeman, C. and Louça, F. (2001). *As time goes by: From the Industrial Revolutions to the Information Revolution*. Oxford, Oxford University Press.

Friends of Europe (2015). *Unequal Europe. Recommendations for a More Caring EU*. Brussels, Friends of Europe.

Galbraith, J. (2012). *Inequality and Instability*. Oxford, Oxford University Press.

Galbraith, J. (2014). Unpacking the first fundamental law. *Real-World Economics Review*, Special issue on Piketty's Capital, 69: 145–9.

Ganzeboom, H. and Treiman, D. (2007). *Ascription and Achievement in Occupational Attainment in Comparative Perspective*. Paper for the Russell Sage-Carnegie University Working Groups on the Social Dimensions of Inequality, Los Angeles, UCLA, 25–26 January 2007.

Gilens, M. and Page B. I. (2014). Testing theories of American politics: Elites, interest groups and average citizens. *Perspectives on Politics*, 12, 3: 564–81.

Glyn, A. (2006). *Capitalism Unleashed*. Oxford, Oxford University Press.

Glyn, A. (2009). Functional distribution and inequality. In Salverda *et al.* (eds), *The Oxford Handbook of Economic Inequality*. Oxford, Oxford University Press, 101–26.

Goldthorpe, J. H. and Jackson, M. (2008). Education-based meritocracy: The barriers to its realisation. In Lareau, A. and Conley, D. (eds), *Social Class: How Does it Work?*. New York, Russell Sage Foundation.

Goos, M. and Manning, A. (2007). Lousy and lovely jobs: The rising polarization of work in Britain. *Review of Economics and Statistics*, 89, 1: 118–33.

Goos, M., Manning, A. and Salomons, A. (2014). Explaining job polarization: Routine-biased technological change and offshoring. *American Economic Review*, 104, 8: 2,509–26.

Gordon, R. (2014). *The Demise of US Economic Growth: Restatement, Rebuttal, and Reflections*, NBER Working Paper 19895. Online: NBER.

Grusky, D. and Kanbur, R. (eds) (2006). *Poverty and Inequality*. Stanford, Stanford University Press.

Hacker, J. S. (2011). *The Institutional Foundation of Middle-Class Democracy*. London, Policy Network.

Hacker, J. and Pierson, P. (2010). *Winner-Take-All Politics. How Washington Made the Rich Richer – and Turned its Back to the Middle Class*. New York, Simon and Schuster.

Hall, S., Massey, D. and Rustin, M. (2015). *After Neoliberalism? The Kilburn Manifesto*. London, Lawrence and Wishart.

Hayter, S. (2015). Unions and collective bargaining. In Berg, J. (ed.), *Labour Markets, Institutions and Inequality: Building Just Societies in the 21st Century*. Geneva and Cheltenham, ILO and Edward Elgar.

Hudson, J. and Sessions, J. (2011). Parental education, labour market experience and earnings: New wine in an old bottle?, *Economics Letters*, 113, 2: 112–15.

ILO (International Labour Office) (2008). *World of Work Report 2008: Income Inequalities in the Age of Financial Globalization*. Geneva, ILO.

ILO (International Labour Office) (2012). *Global Wage Report 2012/13: Wages and Equitable Growth*. Geneva, ILO.

ILO (International Labour Office) (2014). *Global Wage Report 2014/15: Wages and Income Inequalities*. Geneva, ILO.

ILO (International Labour Office) (2015). *World Employment Social Outlook. The Changing Nature of Jobs*. Geneva, ILO.

IMF (International Monetary Fund) (2014). *Fiscal Policy and Income Inequality*. Washington, DC, IMF.

Immervoll, H. and Richardson, L. (2011). *Redistribution Policy and Inequality Reduction in OECD Countries: What has Changed in Two Decades?*, LIS Working Paper Series 571. Luxembourg Income Study.

Intereconomics (2015). Forum: Which industrial policy does Europe need?. *Intereconomics, Review of European Economic Policy*, 50, 3: 120–55.

Jäntti, M. and Jenkins, S. P. (2014). Income mobility. In Atkinson, A. and Bourguignon, F. (eds), *Handbook of Income Distribution*. Amsterdam, Elsevier, 807–935.

Jäntti, M., Sierminska, E. and Smeeding, T. (2008). *The Joint Distribution of Household Income and Wealth: Evidence from the Luxembourg Wealth Study*, OECD Working Paper 65. OECD.

Jappelli, T., Padula, M. and Pica, G. (2010). Do transfer taxes reduce intergenerational transfer?. *Journal of European Economic Association*, 12, 1: 248–75.

Jaumotte, F. and Osorio Buitron, C. (2015). Power from the people. *Finance and Development*, March 2015.

Kaldor, N. (1956). Alternative theories of distribution. *The Review of Economic Studies*, 23, 2: 83–100.

Kalecki, M. (1943). Political aspects of full employment. *Political Quarterly*, 14, 4: 322–31.

Karabarbounis, L. and Neiman, B. (2014). The global decline of the labor share. *Quarterly Journal of Economics*, 129, 1: 61–103.

Katz, L. and Murphy, K. M. (1992). Changes in relative wages, 1963–1987: Supply and demand factors. *Quarterly Journal of Economics*, 107, 1: 35–78.

Kenworthy, L. and Pontusson, J. (2005). Rising inequality and the politics of redistribution in affluent countries. *Perspectives on Politics*, 3, 3: 449–71.

Krueger, A. (2012). *The Rise and Consequences of Inequality in the United States*, Council of Economic Advisers speech, Washington DC, 12 January 2012.

Krugman, P. (2012). *End This Depression Now!*. New York, Norton.

Kuznets, S. (1965). *Economic Growth and Structure: Selected Essays*. London, Heineman.

Lakner, C. and Milanovic, B. (2013). *Global Income Distribution: From the Fall of the Berlin Wall to the Great Recession*, World Bank Policy Research Working Paper 6719, December. Washington, DC, World Bank.

Lansley, S. (2011). *The Cost of Inequality*. London, Gibson Square.

Lapavitsas, C. (2013). *Profiting Without Producing. How Finance Exploits Us All*. London, Verso.

Lavoie, M. and Stockhammer, E. (eds) (2013). *Wage-led Growth: An Equitable Strategy for Economic Recovery*. Geneva and Basingstoke, ILO and Palgrave Macmillan.

Lazonick, W. (2015). *Labor in the Twenty-first Century: The Top 0.1% and the Disappearing Middle Class*, Working Paper 4. New York and online, Institute for New Economic Thinking.

Lazonick, W. and Mazzucato, M. (2013). The risk-reward nexus in the innovation–inequality relationship: Who takes the risks? Who gets the rewards? *Industrial and Corporate Change*, 22, 4: 1093–128.

Lehndorff, S. (ed.) (2015). *Divisive Integration. The Triumph of Failed Ideas in Europe, Revisited*. Brussels, ETUI.

Lemieux, T. (2006). Increasing residual wage inequality: Composition effects, noisy data, or rising demand for skill?. *The American Economic Review*, 96, 3: 461–98.

Levy, F. and Temin, P. (2007). *Inequality and Institutions in 20th Century America*, NBER Working Paper 13106. Online, NBER.

London Health Observatory (2011). *Capital Health Gains?*. London, London Health Observatory.

Lordon, F. (2015). Avec Thomas Piketty, pas de danger pour le capital au XXIe siècle. *Le Monde Diplomatique*, April.

Maddison, A. (2007). *Contours of the World Economy, 1–2030 AD, Essays in Macro-Economic History*. Oxford, Oxford University Press.

Madrick, J. (2011). *Age of Greed, the Triumph of Finance and the Decline of America, 1970–Present*. New York, Knopf.

Maestri, V., Bogliacino, F. and Salverda, W. (2014). Wealth inequality and the accumulation of debt. In Salverda *et al.* (eds), *Changing Inequalities in Rich Countries. Analytical and Comparative Perspectives*. Oxford, Oxford University Press, 82–120.

Marcon, G. and Pianta, M. (2013). *Sbilanciamo l'Economia. Una Via d'Uscita Dalla Crisi*. Rome, Laterza.

Mazzucato, M. (2013a). *The Entrepreneurial State*. London, Anthem.

Mazzucato, M. (2013b). Smart and inclusive growth: Rethinking the State's role and the risk–reward relationship. In Fagerberg, J., Martin, B. and Andersen, E. (eds), *Innovation Studies: Evolution and Future Challenges*. Oxford, Oxford University Press.

Meliciani, V. (2015). *Regional Disparities in the Enlarged EU*. London, Routledge.

Melman, S. (2001). *After Capitalism. From Managerialism to Workplace Democracy*. New York, Knopf.

Milanovic, B. (2005). *Worlds Apart. Measuring International and Global Inequality*. Princeton, Princeton University Press.

Milanovic, B. (2011). *The Haves and the Have-Nots: A Brief and Idiosyncratic History of Global Inequality*. New York, Basic Books.

Milanovic, B. (2012). Global inequality recalculated and updated: The effect of new PPP estimates on global inequality and 2005 estimates. *Journal of Economic Inequality*, 10, 1: 1–18.

Milberg, W. and Winkler, D. (2013). *Outsourcing Economics. Global Value Chains in Capitalist Development*. New York, Cambridge University Press.

Mirowski, P. (2013). *Never let a Serious Crisis Go To Waste. How Neoliberalism Survived the Financial Meltdown*. London, Verso.

Mishel, L. and Davis, A. (2014). *CEO Pay Continues to Rise as Typical Workers are Paid Less*. Issue Brief. Washington, DC, Economic Policy Institute.

Morelli, S., Smeeding, T. and Thompson, J. (2014). Post-1970 trends in within-country inequality and poverty: Rich and middle-income countries. In Atkinson, A. and Bourguignon, F. (eds), *Handbook of Income Distribution*, vol. 2A. Amsterdam, Elsevier, 594–696.

Nascia, L. and Pianta, M. (2009). Forces of inequality? The impact of technology and globalisation. *Intereconomics, Review of European Economic Policy*, 44, 6: 332–6.

OECD (2008). *Growing Unequal? Income Distribution and Poverty in OECD Countries*. Paris, OECD.

OECD (2011). *Divided We Stand. Why Inequality Keeps Rising*. Paris, OECD.

OECD (2012). Labour losing to capital: What explains the declining labour share? *Employment Outlook*. Paris, OECD.

OECD (2014). *All on Board: Making Inclusive Growth Happen*. Paris, OECD.

OECD (2015). *In It Together. Why Less Inequality Benefits All*. Paris, OECD.

Ostry, J. D., Berg, A. and Tsangarides, C. G. (2014). *Redistribution, Inequality, and Growth*, Discussion Note SDN/14/02. Washington, DC, IMF.

Oxfam (2015). *Wealth: Having it all and Wanting More*. London, Oxfam issue briefing.

Pellizzari, M. (2010). Do friends and relatives really help in getting a good job?. *Industrial and Labor Relations Review*, 63, 3: 494–510.

Phillips, K. (2003). *Wealth and Democracy. A Political History of the American Rich*. New York, Broadway Books.

Pianta, M. (2012). *Nove su dieci. Perché stiamo (quasi) tutti peggio di 10 anni fa*. Rome, Laterza.

Pianta, M. (2014). An industrial policy for Europe. *Seoul Journal of Economics*, 27, 3: 277–306.

Pianta, M. and Tancioni, M. (2008). Innovations, wages and profits. *Journal of Post Keynesian Economics*, 31, 1: 101–23.

Pierson, P. and Hacker, J. (2010). *Winner-take-all Politics*. New York, Simon & Schuster.

Piketty, T. (2002). *L'économie des inegalités*. Paris, La Découverte.

Piketty, T. (2013). *Le capital au XXI siècle, Paris, Seuil*. English translation (2014) *Capital in the Twenty-first Century*. Cambridge (Mass.), Harvard University Press.

Piketty, T. (2015). About capital in the twenty-first century. *American Economic Review: Papers & Proceedings*, 105, 5: 48–53.

Piketty, T. and Zucman, G. (2014a). Capital is back: Wealth–income ratios in rich countries 1700–2010. *Quarterly Journal of Economics*, 129, 3: 1,155–210.

Piketty, T. and Zucman, G. (2014b). Wealth and inheritance in the long run. In Atkinson, A. and Bourguignon, F. (eds), *Handbook of Income Distribution*, vol. 2B. Amsterdam, Elsevier, 1,303–68.

Pogge, T. (2002). *World Poverty and Human Rights: Cosmopolitan Responsibilities and Reforms*. Cambridge (UK), Polity Press.

Polanyi, K. (1944). *The Great Transformation*. Boston, Beacon Press.

Pontusson, J. (2005). *Inequality and Prosperity. Social Europe vs. Liberal America*. Ithaca, Cornell University Press.

Raitano, M. and Vona, F. (2011). *Measuring the Link between Inter-generational Occupational Mobility and Earnings: Evidence from Eight European Countries*, OFCE Working Paper 3. Available online: https://ideas.repec.org/f/pra498.html.

Rawls, J. (1971). *A Theory of Justice*. Cambridge (Mass.), Harvard University Press.

Real-World Economics Review (2014). Special Issue on Piketty's *Capital*, 69. World Economics Association.

Robinson, J. (1960). The theory of income distribution. In *Collected Economic Papers*, vol. 2. Oxford, Basil Blackwell, 145–58.

Rodrik, D. (2014). *Good and Bad Inequality*. Social Europe. Available at: www.socialeurope. eu/2014/12/good-bad-inequality/ (accessed July 2015).

Roemer, J. (1998). *Equality of Opportunity*. Cambridge (Mass.), Harvard University Press.

Roemer, J. E. (2004). Equal opportunity and inter-generational mobility: Going beyond inter-generational transition matrices. In Corak, M. (ed.), *Generational Income Mobility in North America and Europe*. Cambridge (UK), Cambridge University Press.

Roemer, J. E. (2009). Inequality: Its justification, nature and domain. In Salverda *et al.* (eds), *The Oxford Handbook of Economic Inequality*. Oxford, Oxford University Press, 23–39.

Rognlie, M. (2015). *Deciphering the Fall and Rise in the Net Capital Share*. Brookings Papers in Economic Activity Conference, 19–20 March.

Rosen, S. (1981). The economics of superstars. *American Economic Review*, 71, 5: 845–58.

Salverda, W. and Checchi, D. (2014). Labor market institutions and the dispersion of wage earnings. In Atkinson, A. and Bourguignon, F. (eds), *Handbook of Income Distribution*, vol. 2B. Amsterdam, Elsevier, 1,536–730.

Salverda, W., Nolan, B. and Smeeding, T. (eds) (2009). *The Oxford Handbook of Economic Inequality*. Oxford, Oxford University Press.

Salverda, W., Nolan, B., Checchi, D., Marx, I., McKnight, A., Tóth, I. and van de Werfhorst, H. (eds) (2014). *Changing Inequalities in Rich Countries. Analytical and Comparative Perspectives*. Oxford, Oxford University Press.

Sbilanciamoci! (2015). *Workers Act. Le politiche per chi lavora e per chi vorrebbe lavorare*. Rome, Sbilanciamoci!.

Schuetz, G., Ursprung, H. and Wößmann, L. (2008). Education policy and equality of opportunity. *Kyklos*, 61, 2: 279–308.

Schulten, T. and Müller, T. (2014). *Back on the Agenda: A European Minimum Wage Standard*. Brussels, ETUI.

Sen, A. (1992). *Inequality Re-examined*. New York, Russell Sage Foundation.

Sen, A. (2000). Social justice and the distribution of income. In: Atkinson, A. and Bourguignon, F. (eds), *Handbook of Income Distribution*, vol. 1. Amsterdam, Elsevier.

Sen, A. (2009). *The Idea of Justice*. Cambridge (Mass.), Harvard University Press.

Sierminska, E., Brandolini, A. and Smeeding, T. (2006). *Comparing Wealth Distribution Across Rich Countries: First Results from the Luxembourg Wealth Study*, LWS Working Paper 1. Luxembourg Wealth Study.

Silver, B. (2003). *Forces of labor. Workers' Movements and Globalization Since 1870*. Cambridge, Cambridge University Press.

Solon, G. (2002). Cross-country differences in inter-generational income mobility. *Journal of Economic Perspectives*, 16, 3: 59–66.

Solow, R. (1956). A contribution to the theory of economic growth. *Quarterly Journal of Economics*, 70, 1: 65–94.

Solow, R. (2014). Thomas Piketty is right. Everything you need to know about *Capital in the Twenty-First Century*. *The New Republic*, 22 April 2014.

Solt, F. (2009). Standardizing the World Income Inequality Database. *Social Science Quarterly*, 90, 2: 231–42.

Stewart, M. B. (2004). The employment effects of the national minimum wage. *Economic Journal*, 114: C110–C116.

Stiglitz, J. (2012). *The Price of Inequality*. New York, Allen Lane.

Stiglitz, J. (2015). *The Great Divide. Unequal Societies and What We Can Do About Them*. New York, Norton.

Sturn, S. and Van Treeck, T. (2013). The role of income inequality as a cause of the Great Recession and global imbalances. In Lavoie, M. and Stockhammer, E. (eds), *Wage-led Growth: An Equitable Strategy for Economic Recovery*. Geneva and Basingstoke, ILO and Palgrave Macmillan, 125–52.

Swaffield, J. K. (2012). *Minimum Wage Hikes and the Wage Growth of Low-wage Workers*, Discussion Papers in Economics 10/12. York, UK: University of York.

Swift, A. (2005). Justice, luck, and the family: The inter-generational transmission of economic advantage from a normative perspective. In Bowles *et al*. (eds), *Unequal Chances: Family Background and Economic Success*. New York, Russell Sage Foundation, 256–76.

Therborn, G. (2013). *The Killing Fields of Inequality*. Cambridge (UK), Polity Press.

UNDP (2014). *Human Development Report 2014*. Geneva, UNDP.

USCEA (United States Council of Economic Advisers) (2014). *The Economic Report of the President Together with the Annual Report of the Council of Economic Advisers, 2014*. Washington, DC, US Government Printing Office.

Uslaner, E. M. (2008). *Corruption, Inequality and the Rule of Law*. New York, Cambridge University Press.

Utting, P., Pianta, M. and Ellersiek, A. (eds) (2012). *Global justice activism and policy reform in Europe. Understanding when change happens*. London, Routledge.

Van Parijs, P. and Vanderborght, Y. (2005). *L'allocation Universelle*. Paris, La Découverte.

Varoufakis, Y. (2014). Egalitarianism's latest foe: A critical review of Thomas Piketty's *Capital in the Twenty-First Century*. *Real-World Economics Review*, 69: 18–35.

Visser, J. and Checchi, D. (2009). Inequality and the labor market: Unions. In Salverda *et al*. (eds), *The Oxford Handbook of Economic Inequality*. Oxford, Oxford University Press, 230–56.

Vivarelli, M. and Pianta, M. (eds) (2000). *The Employment Impact of Innovation*. London, Routledge.

Voitchovsky, S. (2009). Inequality and economic growth. In Salverda *et al*. (eds), *The Oxford Handbook of Economic Inequality*. Oxford, Oxford University Press, 549–74.

Wade, R. H. (2004). Is globalization reducing poverty and inequality? *World Development*, 32, 2: 567–89.

Wade, R. (2014). The Piketty phenomenon and the future of inequality. *Real-World Economics Review*, Special issue on Piketty's *Capital*, 69: 2–17.

Wallerstein, I. (1974). *The Modern World-System*, vol. I. London, Academic Press.

Weil, D. (2015). Capital and wealth in the twenty-first century. *American Economic Review*, 105, 5: 34–7.

Wilkinson, F. and Pickett, K. (2009). *The Spirit Level*. London, Penguin.

World Bank (2006). *World Development Report: Equity and Development*. New York, Oxford University Press.

Zucman, G. (2014). Taxing across borders: Tracking personal wealth and corporate profits. *Journal of Economic Perspectives*, 28, 4: 121–48.

INDEX

References to illustrations are given in italics

Taylor & Francis eBooks

Helping you to choose the right eBooks for your Library

Add Routledge titles to your library's digital collection today. Taylor and Francis ebooks contains over 50,000 titles in the Humanities, Social Sciences, Behavioural Sciences, Built Environment and Law.

Choose from a range of subject packages or create your own!

Benefits for you

» Free MARC records
» COUNTER-compliant usage statistics
» Flexible purchase and pricing options
» All titles DRM-free.

REQUEST YOUR **FREE** INSTITUTIONAL TRIAL TODAY

Free Trials Available
We offer free trials to qualifying academic, corporate and government customers.

Benefits for your user

» Off-site, anytime access via Athens or referring URL
» Print or copy pages or chapters
» Full content search
» Bookmark, highlight and annotate text
» Access to thousands of pages of quality research at the click of a button.

eCollections – Choose from over 30 subject eCollections, including:

Archaeology	Language Learning
Architecture	Law
Asian Studies	Literature
Business & Management	Media & Communication
Classical Studies	Middle East Studies
Construction	Music
Creative & Media Arts	Philosophy
Criminology & Criminal Justice	Planning
Economics	Politics
Education	Psychology & Mental Health
Energy	Religion
Engineering	Security
English Language & Linguistics	Social Work
Environment & Sustainability	Sociology
Geography	Sport
Health Studies	Theatre & Performance
History	Tourism, Hospitality & Events

For more information, pricing enquiries or to order a free trial, please contact your local sales team:
www.tandfebooks.com/page/sales

 **Routledge**
Taylor & Francis Group

The home of
Routledge books

www.tandfebooks.com

For Product Safety Concerns and Information please contact our EU
representative GPSR@taylorandfrancis.com
Taylor & Francis Verlag GmbH, Kaufingerstraße 24, 80331 München, Germany

www.ingramcontent.com/pod-product-compliance
Ingram Content Group UK Ltd.
Pitfield, Milton Keynes, MK11 3LW, UK
UKHW021609240425
457818UK00018B/462